Good Dogs

Good Dogs

HELEN AND GAVIN COOK
FROM THE DOG HOUSE NZ

A Practical Guide to Owning a Happy Dog

ALLEN & UNWIN
AUCKLAND · SYDNEY · MELBOURNE · LONDON

Contents

Introduction It's a dog's life — 9

1 Should you even get a dog? — 35
2 Why get a rescue dog? — 61
3 What sort of dog should you get? — 91
4 Bringing your dog home — 117
5 Sleep — 143
6 Feeding — 165
7 Keeping your dog healthy — 189
8 Keeping your dog happy — 233

Conclusion A friend for life — 285

Introduction

It's a dog's life

There are two types of people in the world: those who have known the love and joy that having a dog can bring to their lives, and those who haven't been lucky enough to experience it yet. I'm among those fortunate people who get to spend pretty much all their time with dogs, and I love them all, big and small. That's just as well, seeing as my whole life revolves around them, from the kennel business I run with my husband, Gavin, to our rescue and sanctuary operation, and our own pet dogs (we currently have four).

When it comes to New Zealand's favourite pets, dogs are second only to cats. More than a third of Kiwi households have a dog. Statistics from Companion Animals New Zealand suggest that in 2020 there were around 850,000 dogs across the country, up from 700,000 in 2011 — and it's probably gone up since then, too, with an increase in pet ownership since the Covid pandemic. Any way you look at it, there are a lot of dogs out there.

There are many different reasons why people get a dog. Sometimes, they're long-term or experienced dog owners who want to add to their pack or find a companion for an older dog, or perhaps their previous pet has passed away and they want to replace it. Some people were brought up with a dog in the family and want their children to have the same experience. Others want a dog for company, or to encourage them to get out and about, take more exercise or be more social. During the pandemic restrictions of the past few years, lots of people seem to have decided to get a dog as something to do, as a bit of entertainment or as a distraction for the kids; this has led to some problems, which I'll talk about later. There are also some significant reasons why people choose to get a rescue dog rather than buy from a breeder or pet shop, and I'll cover those later, too.

Becoming a dog owner — or, really, bringing a dog into your family — is not something to be taken lightly. It's a ten- to fifteen-year commitment for the owner, and a lifetime commitment for the dog. But the love and joy it will bring into your life is unmatched. They say a dog is man's (or woman's) best friend, but it goes deeper than that, and the bond between you and your dog will be one of the closest and most wonderful relationships you can experience. Dogs love human company and bond very closely with those who care for them, which is why I do what I do. I believe every dog deserves a safe, comfortable and loving home, and I am so pleased to play a part in that process through the Country Retreat Animal Sanctuary.

I've written this book not only as a practical guide to keeping a canine companion, but also as a tribute to the wonderful owners and volunteers we have worked with who put so much time, effort and love into taking care of the dogs and puppies that we rescue. We hope you enjoy reading their stories as well as learning more about what makes dogs tick and how to give them the best possible life.

A bit about dogs . . .

Our relationship with dogs goes back a long way. They first became domesticated more than 15,000 years ago — before the development of agriculture, when people were still hunter-gatherers. They're actually the only large carnivore species that has ever become a domestic animal — the only living thing capable of killing and eating us that we allow to live in our homes! You might not think of it this way when your beloved pooch is

Dog breeds

Today's grey wolves have the Latin name *Canis lupus*. All domestic dogs — despite the massive differences in size, shape, colour and coat among modern breeds — are the same species: *Canis lupus familiaris*, usually shortened to *Canis familiaris* — which translates as 'canid belonging to the family or household'.

The huge number of breeds we see today — more than 220 are recognised by Dogs New Zealand (formerly the New Zealand Kennel Club) — is a fairly recent development. Although dogs have come in different sizes and shapes, to fill different roles, for hundreds of years, it's only been in the past couple of centuries that standards for specific breeds have been recognised based on looks and physical characteristics.

The first breeds to be officially recognised in the US and UK were types of setter, spaniel, pointer, terrier and hound in the 1870s and 1880s. Breeders brought together dogs with traits and physical characteristics they desired to produce the 'ideal' dog of its type. One example is the bull terrier. As its name suggests, this came about from breeding old-style British terrier dogs with bulldogs and also Dalmatians, to produce the white coat favoured by fashionable gentlemen, once the dog stopped being bred for fighting and became a desirable companion.

Despite all the differences, dogs know — just as we do — when another animal is a dog. In fact, I don't think dogs pay any attention to size or type; to them, a dog is a dog! When two dogs meet and greet, they are more attuned to each other's personality and manner than what each looks like or what breed they are.

curled up on the couch after a trip to the groomer, but when you live with a dog, you are continuing a deeply ingrained human behaviour which began when grey wolves — the ancestors of all today's dogs — first began to live closely alongside us.

Wolves are naturally wary creatures. But some of those early wolves would have been more prepared than others to cosy up to early humans, in exchange for food and warmth. In return, those humans would utilise the wolves' hunting and guarding skills. This mutually beneficial relationship would have led some wolves — or early dogs, we might call them — to throw in their lot with wandering bands of hunter-gatherers. Some experts believe that in this way dogs actually *domesticated themselves*. They chose to live with us because it suited them, just as it suited our ancestors to keep a dog around the camp.

Throughout the thousands of years that have passed since wolves started sharing the warmth of human fires, we have selectively bred specific qualities into domestic dogs to make them less like their ancestors and more like the pet animals we know today. For example, today's dogs are well known for their ability to express emotion on their faces and communicate with their gaze — they don't call it 'puppy eyes' for nothing — whereas wolves can't even move their eyebrows. Having an expressive face is a feature that we have either subconsciously or consciously bred into the dogs we live with today, which is why we feel like they are listening to us or empathising with us.

However, up until a few hundred years ago, most dogs were bred and kept for their usefulness, rather than purely as companions. As the majority of the population were working people, the vast majority of dogs were working dogs. Dogs have long been used for hunting and retrieving game; for guarding other domestic animals such as sheep, and protecting people and property; and for pulling loads, like sled dogs in the Arctic. Only the very rich could afford to have dogs purely as pets (although some did have little jobs — the lion-faced shih tzu was kept by Chinese noble families and carried around inside their robes like a portable heater).

Different breeds were developed according to their physical characteristics, to suit the work they did. Dogs with waterproof coats and strong swimming ability were used to retrieve waterfowl. Poodles, for instance, were originally bred as duck-hunting dogs — their fancy-looking coat clip was originally to minimise the amount of hair that got wet, while keeping their joints warm. Some dogs served as fierce-looking guardians which would raise the alarm or deal with intruders; some breeds would grab and hold intruders, biting them hard to put them out of action, while others, like the bull mastiff, might pull them to the ground and sit on them until help arrived. In medieval Europe, hardy little dogs were used almost like a piece of machinery, running in a wheel that turned a spit for cooking meat.

Kurī

Māori also originally had dogs, which they brought from Polynesia to Aotearoa on their waka when they settled here. These kurī, which are now extinct, were small, with pale fur that was prized and made into prestigious cloaks for chiefs. They did not bark, but made a howling noise that Māori described as 'auau'. As well as helping with hunting, kurī were also used as food themselves (James Cook ate one on his first voyage here). They gradually died out as a separate type through interbreeding with European dogs in the early nineteenth century.

A bit about us

Gavin and I have both had a long journey to where we are now, running the Country Retreat boarding kennels and animal sanctuary. Both of us are originally from North East England, although we've lived in New Zealand for more than thirty years. I met Gavin when he was the best man at my friend's wedding; my little daughter, Emma, was a flower girl, and they came down the aisle hand in hand. It must have been a sign, because we've been together ever since! We married in 1989 and our son, Anthony, was born in 1990, six years after I'd had Emma.

We decided that we wanted to emigrate, because where we were living wasn't a great area to bring up kids. We wanted them to be able to see a different future and to have more opportunities as they grew up. We looked at a few different places, but New Zealand really appealed, and we qualified under the immigration points system. Gavin had never even been in a plane

before, and my only overseas experience had been a one-week holiday in Crete. But off we went, with two kids aged three and eight, and five suitcases, and our first week's accommodation in Auckland booked. Beyond that, who knew what would happen?

We found a place to live in Mt Roskill, and both of us found jobs pretty easily. I went into a shop to buy some shoes and was offered a part-time job there. Gavin got a full-time role at Fisher & Paykel, and we moved over to the North Shore and bought a house in Torbay. We worked as hard as we could to get ahead once the kids were a bit older: I had three part-time jobs, and Gavin worked full-time and did lots of overtime. Having left school at the age of sixteen, I also went back to school and did a degree in early childhood education.

My nana gave me my first dog, Judy, a Schnauzer. My nana was given this dog as part of a debt owed to her. She also had a German shepherd called Rebel, an ex-police dog who didn't like people in uniform. He was a great guard dog for the pub we lived in that my nana managed. I was terrified of dogs, to the extent that I would run out onto the road if I saw one coming down the footpath towards me. But this dog Nana got me, Judy, was amazing, and completely cured me of my fear of dogs. She used to escape from home and come and meet me walking home from school a mile away.

My parents didn't particularly like animals, and neither did my brother. I really wanted a Dalmatian, but eventually I wore my parents down and they got me a Jack Russell — my parents always joked that they could only afford one spot! To be honest, this dog was an absolute terror that wanted to attack anything that came near it. It didn't like any dog bigger than it was — which was pretty much any other dog. That probably came about because my parents would pull it away from any other dogs they met, so it became lead-aggressive. Gavin had a bit more luck: he was brought up with dogs, although he does complain that everything in his life was female. He was brought up by his mum and had two sisters, then they had two female dogs, and a rabbit that was female as well!

When we first got together in the UK, we didn't have a dog of our own because we were so busy with work and other commitments. But once we emigrated and moved to our house in Torbay, we were finally able to get

our own dog, Fern. She was a mastiff–boxer cross from the SPCA, but she became very protective of me and aggressive towards other people. Sadly, despite consulting several trainers, we made the tough decision to have her put to sleep, as her behaviour had become dangerous.

Anthony and I had been attacked by a German shepherd when Anthony was little, and it had left both of us feeling very wary of dogs. We didn't want him to grow up being scared of dogs like I had been, so we persisted. Our next dog, Muttley, was a German shepherd cross, and Anthony wouldn't go near him for about a month, but then they became best buddies. Muttley was pretty stubborn and would tolerate other dogs for only a short time, but he and Anthony were great mates.

One day we went to get him a collar from the pet shop and saw another dog there, and came home with a mastiff–ridgeback cross. We called her Ebony, and she ended up weighing 47 kg! She matched our daughter's personality — so laid back she was just about falling over. Whenever we went to the park, she'd just lie down and Emma would use her as a pillow and read a book, while Anthony and Muttley would be running around! We also had a third dog, Peggy, who was a Dalmatian–Staffy cross.

Muttley lived for sixteen years, although he developed arthritis in his old age. Ebony never had any problems, but then she got lymphoma and died at the age of eleven. Emma was away when she died, and she was heartbroken. Peggy, sadly, also died of cancer. The kids had grown up with these dogs, and even though they were now adults, it was very hard to say goodbye to their old pets.

When the kids were a bit older, we had moved out to a 5-acre section at Kaukapakapa, north of Auckland. At last, we were able to fulfil our dream of fostering rescue dogs until permanent homes could be found for them. We took on puppies and specialised in fostering bully breeds — dogs that other people might be too scared or too prejudiced to look after — for North Auckland Dog Rescue and Bridge Bully Rescue.

We also got another dog of our own after Ebony died, a pit bull–mastiff cross called Bella, so we had three dogs, a blue-tongued lizard called Gizmo and some chickens. I've always been a bit of a collector of animals that other people don't want or have tried to throw away, and that's continued with the sanctuary.

When Muttley passed away, we took on another rescue who was fear-aggressive (he would lunge at you if he was scared): a mastiff–Great Dane cross called Zeus. As you can probably imagine, he was a big boy and he needed muzzling in public, but we worked with him to manage his fear and he was lovely when he knew you and felt comfortable with you.

We also took on a white fluffy thing called Dorothy (Dot for short), who came from a backyard breeder. After all the big mastiff cross types we'd had, I was quite attracted to the idea of having a smaller dog, as I used to get pins and needles when the bigger dogs sat in my lap! I thought it would be nice to have a little dog that would cuddle me, but it hasn't worked out like that — she's not a lap dog, and the big ones still sit on me. Despite her looks, Dot is a proper little farm dog who likes riding around on the quad bike with Gavin.

Our rescue operation and sanctuary

We wanted to extend our place at Kaukapakapa but couldn't get council permission. In 2014, I was working as a private caregiver and Gavin had an HR management position, but we were asking ourselves, is this really what we want to do? We both wanted to work for ourselves, so Gavin suggested we look at buying a boarding kennel. I basically went out that weekend, saw what is now Country Retreat, and started the process of buying it the same day. I couldn't have told you anything about the house, as I was concentrating on the facilities for dogs, which says a lot about me! I could see it was a place where we could both run the kennels as a business and set up a rescue operation as well, so I could go on helping dogs that needed to find a home. We started off small, but we always had plans to make it bigger and better. (In February 2020, we would become a registered charity.)

In 2019, we bought around 3.2 hectares of land adjacent to our property which couldn't otherwise be accessed, and, after negotiating a lot of red tape, got permission from the council to set up an animal sanctuary. We started by converting the garage into a proper puppy home, getting it fully lined and insulated, then saved up to have a concrete slab put down and build a series of 'pods' where we could keep groups of dogs, each with their own little outdoor area and a place to eat and sleep. This wasn't cheap: it cost $35,000 just to get electricity to the new power pole, another $20,000 to get it from the pole to the pods, then another $60,000 to build the pods. Most of the money we put into the rescue operation comes from the profit from our kennel business, but as a registered charity we also receive donations and have people sponsor us every week — even the price of a coffee donated to us can make a big difference. We get such amazing support; we couldn't do it without our community.

Unfortunately, our buying the property and starting work on expanding the rescue operation coincided with the first Covid lockdowns. We had to shut down our kennel business, and the animal shelters grew frantic, trying to find places for dogs to go. Lots of dogs were being put to sleep. We knew of people who had said they would take dogs and help foster before Covid, but it wasn't always possible to arrange, and we ended up with twenty-six dogs living in our house! We had no money coming in, and any savings we had went into keeping the sanctuary going . . . It was a very tough time.

It wasn't all about money, either; it was mentally tough as well. Sadly, Zeus became quite sick with cancer during the lockdowns, and we spent around $10,000 trying to help him before making the hard decision to have him put down. I was heartbroken and felt like I would never want another dog again. I told Gavin we'd just have Dot and do rescues and that was it — no more dogs of our own.

I'm sure it won't surprise you to hear that it was less than a year before things changed. I'd been to the council shelters a few times to collect pregnant dogs to bring back to the sanctuary, and I kept seeing this dog that no one seemed to want to take home — probably because she was so big, and so full-on, and seemed like she would be really hard to control. Well . . . next thing you know, I'm taking her home with me. So then we had another big dog: Agnes, a wire-haired pointer–mastiff cross. She's about 47 kg, and when she came to us she'd had no real training. She found our cats a little *too* interesting; they love one another now, but for the first two weeks we had to keep her on a lead at all times so she didn't try to chase and play with them.

The people at the pound knew that I had a soft spot for mastiffs, and they had one come in with cherry eye, which is when the third eyelid gland pops out onto the white part of the eye. This gland produces a lot of the moisture that the dog's eyes need, and while it's not necessarily painful for the dog, the red, swollen mass needs to be surgically corrected by a vet, and can be quite expensive to fix. I took her home with me the first day I met her! We named her Penny and she ended up needing five operations to fix her eye, but we love her. She weighed about 60 kg when she was around a year old — and she was still growing.

At this point I said, seriously, no more dogs . . . but then one of our kennel customers was looking for a home for her dog, which had stayed with us a few times. She was looking to travel long-term and was wanting him to be rehomed, either by surrendering the dog to us or offering him back to the breeder — he was a pure-bred St Bernard. We don't take many voluntary surrenders, because there are so many rescues that need homes and are otherwise facing being put down. But I was so in love with this dog

from when he had stayed with us in the kennels that I couldn't resist. I've never had a pure-bred dog before and he is just beautiful (although a little slobbery!). His name is Jeffrey, and at the time of writing he weighs around 80 kg (and is also still growing).

Just in case you think we're dog-mad, we also have the two cats: Tinker, who's the boss, and Oscar, who's a real smoocher. We inherited them from a friend who'd moved to a property where she couldn't take them. I'd never had cats before, but they fitted in well, and we've had them for nine years now. Neither of them minds the dogs — they'll just give them a swipe of the paw to put them in their place if they're any bother, and often they'll all curl up to sleep together.

The sanctuary has grown from its early origins, and now we are licensed to have fifty dogs and puppies at a time, in our pod units and the puppy house in the original garage. We have a large exercise yard, and we've added a new building which includes an office for me and space for the older dogs and ones that need extra TLC if they are sick or injured. As well as rescue dogs, we've now got goats, ducks, pigs, sheep, chickens, cats and peacocks in our sanctuary.

My next plan is to build a cattery, and I would also like to create a special fenced space at the sanctuary where people can bring their dogs to have some safe off-lead time. This would be good for dogs that can't be let off-leash in other areas for whatever reason — they react to other dogs, for example — or for group doggy play-dates.

Gavin and I are the only people who work full-time in the sanctuary (without being paid), and we also have a fantastic team of volunteers — we couldn't do it without them. We also have amazing support from sponsors, members of the public and suppliers, such as J-Spec, Rhodes for Roads, Pet Direct, Purina, Fonko, Temperzone, Coast Pet Care, Mitre 10, Refspecs and Promac.

Rescuing dogs and rehoming them is a real team effort, and we hope to be able to go on giving dogs a second chance at life for a long time to come.

Ryan and Christine adopted pit bull cross Lily, one of the sanctuary's great success stories, in 2021, when she was around two years old. In early 2023, they added the adorable Abby (formerly Vera) to their pack.

Christine: I always knew that when the time came, we would adopt. Ryan had always grown up with dogs, and Lily was our first dog together.

Ryan works full-time from home, and we had room for a companion for him. I originally trained as a vet nurse, and know first-hand how important adopting is. It also means not giving money to puppy mills, while supporting great organisations like Country Retreat.

Puppies are cute, but they always get homed and older dogs tend to get overlooked. For this reason, I really wanted someone special, someone older. We had been following Lily's story online for some time — giving birth to puppies and eventually coming up for adoption herself. I reached out to my friend who works at the kennels there to enquire about Lily. She replied we *had* to meet her. It was almost love at first sight — Lily went straight to Ryan to say hello, he sat down on the ground beside her and they both began rolling around together, cuddling. She's definitely a daddy's girl.

Ryan: Lily had spent some time at Country Retreat and had had some training. However, it got to the point where she was very dependent on me.

We went through a phase when she didn't cope with being left at home — she developed bad separation anxiety. We started talking about getting her a companion, another dog she could hang out with. By now we had a larger country section and knew we could offer another rescue a home, as well as get Lily a companion.

Christine: We set up several meet-and-greets with dogs, most of whom Lily wasn't interested in. But then Abby came up online, so we enquired about her. Helen picked it: she said, 'They will take her home.'

Lily was very excited to meet Abby, and there was an instant connection. She was the first dog that Lily had really interacted with, and that's what we were looking for, and what really made the decision for us.

Abby is a bit of a sook, a mummy's girl. I'd wanted something a bit smaller, but I now have a 20 kg lap dog! Lily is naturally chill, but Abby gets the zoomies. Abby is a bit more high-energy so she annoys Lily every now and then: the big sister–little sister thing. They like playing tag and chasing each other — they get on really well.

Ryan: It's really good for Lily, as she doesn't spend time with me any more — she's busy doing dog things. They're both more settled, hanging out in the sun somewhere.

Lily was easy to train. She's very food- and praise-driven. We've done a lot of training with her — basic things, building her confidence. She does well with routines and boundaries, whereas Abby likes to challenge them a bit. Abby thrives on positive reinforcement — she doesn't like being told off!

Lily's main issue is a lack of confidence, whereas Abby has a little too much at times. She is very social, and if she sees another dog or a person she has to go and say hi, whereas Lily will say hi but then go off and do her own thing. Abby is a real character.

Christine: The idea of breaking the cycle of dogs being abandoned is important to us, and I always knew I would get a rescue. There's something special about them, as well as the idea of helping. You get a dog off the street and give them a new life. It can be a lot of work, but you have given them another chance — especially with a dog like Lily, who had had such a sad story. She probably would have been put down, and she's such a lovely dog.

Helen says:

In 2020, we were contacted by a council animal control branch, desperate for our help. They were looking for a home for a pit bull cross named Lily, who had been abandoned in a desolate paddock. A compassionate farmer had spotted her and provided temporary shelter until the local pound could intervene.

Lily's fate teetered on a precipice. The stigma around 'bully breeds' means they are often hard to find homes for, and they can be unjustly put down if left at the pound.

We embarked on a gruelling journey to collect her, driving for over five hours in heavy traffic. When we finally laid eyes on Lily, she crawled towards us on her stomach, frightened and scarred by her earlier treatment, but desperately wanting to trust again.

We could tell that Lily had suffered greatly. Her emaciated frame told a tale of starvation and neglect, and she had a festering sore on her back. Even though it was on a public holiday, we arranged for a vet to see her, knowing that she needed immediate attention, starting with antibiotics to combat the infection.

As I lifted her fragile form and coaxed her into a slow, trembling walk towards the veterinary clinic, a stranger stopped us. In an act of extraordinary kindness, she contributed $100 towards Lily's veterinary bills.

Lily's condition was dire. Vaccinations had to be postponed due to her weakened state, so we focused on treating her open wounds with antiseptic cream. Her engorged teats, hard as rocks, hinted at both recent motherhood and severe mastitis. We bathed her gently, freeing her from the filth that clung to her weakened body. We gave her worm and flea treatment, and a nourishing meal. Eventually she fell asleep in my arms. Every time I attempted to move, she stirred, seeking comfort and security.

We initially dismissed the possibility of her being pregnant, believing her swollen teats were a sign that she had recently had a litter. However, x-rays revealed the truth — Lily was indeed carrying new life, in the early stages. With her condition in mind, we adjusted her medications and made sure she received the food and care a pregnant mother needs.

One of the vets warned that she might need a C-section to deliver her puppies, due to their size, so we closely monitored Lily as the time drew near for her to give birth. She eventually gave birth naturally to eight puppies.

Lily proved to be an extraordinary mother, protective of her offspring. Initially, she permitted only me to come near them. On one occasion when I had to go out briefly, Gavin reported that Lily had tucked her babies under my desk, guarding them with fierce devotion.

The toll on Lily's body was evident — her infected mammary glands swelled, rigid with pain, and she panted incessantly. Course after course of antibiotics, anti-inflammatories, painkillers and cool-packs became our arsenal in the battle to ease her discomfort.

At four weeks old, the pups had to be separated from Lily, as her milk showed signs of infection. We took on the task of hand-rearing her babies while we tried alternative antibiotics, but the lumps in her mammaries persisted. Consultations with the vet led to a difficult decision — we would wait a few more weeks to see if there was any improvement, and if none came, surgery would be the only option. Miraculously, the lumps diminished significantly, and we continued treatment until they finally vanished.

For four months, Lily underwent intensive treatment, then the time came for her to be spayed and go to a new home. However, finding the perfect home for a pit bull cross presented its own challenges. We dedicated ourselves to training Lily, teaching her how to interact with other dogs. She learned house manners, mastered basic commands, and even acquired a repertoire of tricks. With three daily exercise sessions among a pack of dogs, Lily thrived.

Christine and Ryan took a leap of faith when they decided to adopt Lily. But Lily, true to her incredible nature, exceeded all expectations. They loved Lily's vibrant spirit and playful nature, and the way she showered them with unconditional love and endless tail wags.

In 2023, Christine and Ryan came back to us to adopt a friend for Lily, so we introduced them to Vera (renamed Abby). With her little upturned nose and teeth adorably sticking out, Abby's charm was irresistible.

Lily, true to her nature, warmly welcomed Abby into their home. The two dogs formed an inseparable bond, embarking on adventures together, playing chase in the backyard, and snuggling up for cosy naps.

1

Should you even get a dog?

There are a lot of factors to weigh up before deciding to get a dog, whether it's a puppy or an adult dog, a rescue from an animal shelter or sanctuary, or a dog from a breeder. There are so many advantages and wonderful benefits to be gained from having a dog in your life, but dog ownership is a significant commitment, and you and everyone in your family needs to do some serious thinking before taking one on. Those scenes you see in movies when Daddy comes home with a puppy with a bow around its neck and everyone is so surprised and excited? Please don't do that! If everyone gave adequate thought and consideration to getting a dog before taking that step, there would be much less need for rescues and sanctuaries like ours. Obviously, sometimes dog owners' circumstances change beyond their control — they have to relocate, they become sick or pass away, and so on — but many dogs end up dumped because their owners didn't think it through properly, or just don't want to look after them any more.

Owning a dog is certainly more of a commitment than having a cat or other pets. You don't have to exercise a cat or a rabbit; they're quite happy doing their own thing for hours on end, and they're easy for someone else to take care of and feed if you are away. Dogs also need training and socialising if you want them to survive in the world outside your home. Dogs need to be regularly exercised and mentally stimulated. Dogs need much more time and attention than any other pet.

The time and effort you put into a dog will pay off hugely — but if you don't put in that time and love and effort in the first six months, quite frankly your dog will probably end up being a little horror! From day one of taking that dog or puppy home, you need to set down the rules and boundaries and stick to them. If you show it love and care and consistency, a dog will be the most loyal, loving companion you could ever hope for.

Benefits

Dog ownership can have a significant impact on your lifestyle. But before we look at some of the potential downsides or responsibilities it brings, what about the benefits? Here are some key advantages of having a dog in your life:

- **Dogs make wonderful companions.** This is probably the main reason for most owners. Having an animal sharing your home, but especially a dog, creates a special relationship. They know that you are the person who cares for them and provides the things they need, and in return you are the recipient of their unconditional love and devotion. A dog is by nature a pack animal, and it feels happiest when it is with the people it belongs to (and who belong to it). Your dog never has something else to do when you want to hang out with it — being with you is its favourite thing in the world. Unlike cats, which can be a bit choosy as to when they want to hang out, dogs are literally adapted by evolution to be a companion to humans: they feel happiest when they're right by your side (and not only when you're eating), or at least somewhere near you. Dogs can be great companions if you're feeling sick, too, staying by your side and keeping an eye on you. It makes me really sad and angry when I see people abuse or take advantage of that bond of loyalty by mistreating or chaining their dog, abandoning them or leaving them alone for long periods. It just makes me sick, and it's one of the reasons Gavin and I get so much satisfaction from finding forever homes for dogs that have been rescued. We know from experience how wonderful it is to be welcomed home by a dog with a wagging tail and a loving lick.

- **They're good for your physical health.** It's very hard to have a dog and be inactive — if you spend too much time sitting around, and not enough time walking and playing, your dog will let you know all about it! Rain or shine, whether you feel like exercising or not, your dog is always up for it. Even small or low-energy dogs need regular exercise to keep them physically fit and healthy and mentally stimulated. Even if you don't have a working dog that needs to go for regular runs, taking your dog for a decent walk every day, even if it's just around the block for half an hour, will keep you fit and have an impact on your cardiovascular health. One study showed that dog owners on average walked twenty-two minutes more per day than people who didn't own a dog — and at a reasonable pace, too. Other studies have also shown that dog owners are more likely to engage in regular physical activity, eat healthier diets and have better blood sugar levels; another showed that adults who regularly walked their dogs were less likely to be obese. Walking for thirty minutes a day has been shown to reduce your risk of coronary heart disease, osteoporosis, colon and breast cancer, and Type 2 diabetes — and help you sleep better, too. If you can't get out and about, then playing fetch or tug of war at home, or just chasing the dog to get your stolen socks back, can also count as exercise!

- **They're good for your mental health, too.** There are so many aspects of dog ownership which have a positive impact on your mental well-being. Regardless of what else is going on in your day, seeing your dog's happy face and spending time petting or playing with it is bound to make you feel better. Dogs are so in the moment, it's hard to feel down around them. Dogs are also good for keeping us motivated, which can be lacking

if we are feeling a bit down — they thrive on routine, so having a canine companion can give you the push you need to keep going with regular activities, including exercise, which is a massive mood-booster and can help reduce stress and anxiety.

- **They help us to be more social.** Anyone who has taken a dog for a walk will know that other people are much more likely to say hello than if you were on your own, and they'll even stop for a pat and a chat. When out and about with your pooch, especially at the park or beach or places where there are other dogs, you will meet other dog owners and enthusiasts, and often end up having conversations with them. You will get to know the other dog owners in your neighbourhood, and it might even lead to organised doggy play-dates. Even if you are shy or introverted, having your dog with you can increase your sense of connection, especially when other people smile at you. And even if you are out without your dog, you may find you strike up conversations with other dog owners.

- **They provide a sense of security.** Dogs are utterly loyal to their pack, which means you and your family. Even if your dog isn't large or fierce-looking, like a regular 'guard' dog, it still has a natural protective instinct and will alert you to any potential dangers. When you take your dog for walks, just having it with you can make you feel safer and more confident. Also, having a dog in your house or on your property can act as a deterrent against burglaries and intruders — even a little dog barking a lot is likely to draw attention and put off anyone who is up to no good.

- **They are emotionally supportive.** Dogs have an exceptional ability to sense and respond to human emotions. They are so sensitive to human feelings, they can tell when you're sad or upset, and will often come to you to offer comfort and check that you are OK. They're also someone to talk to — even if they can't talk back, they provide a sympathetic ear, especially if you are stroking them at the same time. Dogs can provide genuine comfort and emotional support during challenging times and feelings of stress, anxiety or loneliness. Just being the centre of someone's world, and seeing it in their shining eyes, is a mood-booster for a start! The simple act of petting or cuddling your dog also releases oxytocin, a hormone associated with relaxation and stress reduction; in fact, when you and your dog stare into each other's eyes, it releases oxytocin in both your brain and the dog's, increasing the bond between you and making you both feel 'warm fuzzies'.

They encourage responsibility. Caring for a dog makes us accountable, and can be a super-positive way for older kids to gain a greater sense of responsibility. Caring for another living being requires setting routines for feeding, exercise, grooming and regular vet visits. Taking on these responsibilities can help develop important life skills and foster a sense of empathy and compassion. We can all benefit from thinking about something other than ourselves, and you will gain a lot of satisfaction from taking good care of your dog and making sure it is happy and its needs are being met.

As you can see, owning a dog offers numerous benefits. Dogs truly enrich our lives and become cherished members of our families, bringing joy, love and entertainment. Once you've had a dog, you may find it hard to imagine life without one.

Potential downsides

The biggest potentially negative factor to consider is the long-term commitment that comes with dog ownership — it's not just a matter of 'let's get a dog, that'll be fun'. Dogs are not temporary friends; they are lifelong companions. When you bring a dog into your home, you are committing to being responsible for their well-being and care for their entire lifespan, which can be up to fifteen years or more, from the challenges of puppyhood through their 'teenage' years and on to being an adult and then senior dog.

Their needs, energy levels and health will change, and you will have to be there for them every step of the way.

So for the next fifteen years of your life, you've got to be able to look after and care for your dog *every day*. That's something you really have to think about — for the next fifteen years you can't just go on holiday! It doesn't mean you can never go away ever again, or never even leave the house, but it does mean you have to be prepared to find a way for your dog to be cared for if you are away from home for more than a couple of hours, in some cases, and certainly overnight. There is usually a cost associated with that, whether that's putting the dog in kennels or a 'dog hotel', boarding at someone's house, or getting someone to stay with the dog at your own place. And that also means you have to have a dog that can tolerate other dogs and behave itself around other people.

As a responsible dog owner, you have a duty to provide for your dog's physical and emotional needs. This includes good food, a comfortable home, and regular visits to the vet for vaccinations, check-ups and when it becomes sick or injured. This all comes at a financial cost (see below) as well as being a time commitment.

Regular physical exercise is crucial for a dog's overall well-being, no matter what its breed and size. Mental stimulation and play are vital, too, to stop the dog becoming bored and destructive. Socialising and training are also essential to prevent behavioural issues and ensure your dog's safety. And being a responsible dog owner also means picking up poo, to ensure a healthy environment at home and out and about.

Overall, dog ownership requires time, effort and resources, both physical and in terms of time, and you need to make sure you consider all the factors before taking one on.

The cost of ownership

The cost of dog ownership extends beyond the initial purchase or adoption fee. When you first get a dog, it will need to be registered, vaccinated, microchipped and definitely desexed, if it isn't already.

In New Zealand, the basic average cost of dog ownership is approximately $1500 per year — and that's just the bare basics of food and annual vaccinations, excluding any extras like grooming, daycare or boarding, additional veterinary requirements or pet insurance. It is important to budget for these ongoing expenses to ensure you can provide proper care for your dog and maintain their well-being.

Ongoing expenses include:

- **Food:** All dogs require regular feeding on a balanced diet that meets their nutritional needs. What you choose to feed your dog will affect the cost — raw feeding is much more expensive than dry food or dog roll (see pages 165–177) — as, of course, will the size of your dog and how much it eats. As a very general guide, a 10kg bag of good-quality dog kibble costs around $120 and would feed a medium-sized dog for about a month.

- **Flea and worm treatments** (see page 195): Regular flea, worm and tick treatments are essential for maintaining your dog's health and preventing infestations. An all-round flea and worm treatment costs around $30 a month.

- **Registration:** In New Zealand, all dog owners are legally required to register their pets with local authorities. The annual fee for this varies by council, but can be up to around $200 in the main centres, and less in provincial centres and rural areas.

- **Vaccinations:** Puppies need a full course of initial vaccinations, and adult dogs need regular boosters to protect them against various diseases (see page 194). The cost is around $100 a year.

- **Grooming:** Some breeds of dogs may require regular professional grooming, which can add up to several hundred dollars a year, depending on your dog's coat and how often it needs to be clipped or groomed.

- 🐾 **Daycare or boarding:** If you work outside the home or go on holiday, you will need to arrange for daycare or boarding services. In Auckland, daycare can cost up to around $50 a day, with a little extra for overnight stays — but again, costs can vary.

- 🐾 **Additional veterinary requirements and dog insurance:** You never know when your dog is going to need to see the vet. Emergency consultations cost even more than regular consultations. These costs can vary greatly depending on the dog's health needs but can add up very quickly, especially if medications, imaging and/or surgery are required. Having pet insurance will cover some but not all of these costs, and of course you have to pay regular premiums.

Is my lifestyle suited to a dog?

Not everyone's way of life is suited to dog ownership. If you work long hours, are away frequently, lived in shared accommodation, have very small children or are planning to leave New Zealand in the next few years, this might not be the right time to get a dog. As I've said above, it's a commitment for the lifetime of the dog — so you need to have some idea that your lifestyle is going to be reasonably stable and you will be able to provide it with a good home over the long term.

You don't necessarily need to be in your own home, or be a mature adult, to be a dog owner. Many young people get dogs that suit their busy, active lifestyles and have a ball with them — but they have to be committed to maintaining that caring relationship into the future. Also, older adults can enjoy the companionship of a dog in their later years, but it's probably better to get an older dog, too, which needs less exercise and stimulation and won't be left 'orphaned' at a young age, rather than a puppy.

Here are some factors you need to take into account when considering if you're in the right stage of your life to take on dog ownership:

- 🐾 **Where are you living?** Do you own your own home, or are you renting? If you have your own home, you have a much greater degree of control over the physical environment your dog would live in, especially in terms of fencing, and are responsible only to yourself for any damage the dog might do to the house and grounds; plus you have more power over when and where you might move. Being in a rental property doesn't mean you can't get a dog — your landlord may be agreeable to it — but you have much less control. The person who owns your property might not want to pay for improving fencing and gates, and if the dog damages the property, by chewing on woodwork or ruining the carpets, for example, you may lose some of your bond. You also might have to move with a minimum of notice and struggle to find somewhere else that will take you and your dog.

- 🐾 **What sort of property are you living in?** The ideal situation is for the dog to have access to a safe, fenced outdoor area with shelter — preferably a garden, but a decent-sized deck will do. I believe domestic dogs should live primarily inside, and be allowed access to the main living areas so they can spend time with you and feel like part of the family. Just because you live in a small house or apartment doesn't mean you can't get a dog, but it might affect the type of dog you choose to get, and you may need to take them out more often for exercise and stimulation.

- 🐾 **What sort of fencing does it have?** Being able to keep your dog on your property is absolutely critical, so it is not able to roam and run the risk of being hit by a car, impounded or even stolen, and so it cannot get into trouble with the neighbours. If you live in a city or town, your back section at least should be fully fenced, with secure gates. If you live rurally, you will still need to have a safe, fenced area for the dog to be in when you are not at home. You may need to revisit your fencing situation if your dog is a jumper or a digger. Leaving your dog tied or chained up when you are out is both cruel and dangerous — it is not able to get itself away from any danger or threats, and it could be strangled or choked if the tether gets caught on something.

- **What is your living situation?** Are you living alone, as a couple, with your family, or in a sharing situation like a flat? Does everyone in the house want to get a dog? If you have very small children, you will need to think carefully about what sort of dog you get, and always be extremely careful: never leave children and dogs together unsupervised (see pages 49–51). Some people find it no problem to juggle having a new dog and a new baby, but if you are at that stage of your life it might be more fair on the dog to wait at least until the intense baby phase is over.

- **What is your daily routine and/or work situation?** Most dogs can handle some time alone, but dogs are social animals and do require companionship. Think about your daily routine and how much time the dog would have to spend alone. If you work long hours or have frequent commitments outside the home, it may not be fair to leave a dog alone for extended periods. If you have to pay for regular daycare or for someone else to walk your dog or take it on outings, that can really add up financially. Dogs left alone for too long can experience loneliness and anxiety and develop behavioural problems — as a lot of people found when they went back to work once the Covid lockdowns were over. Dogs also like routine, so if you keep irregular hours, are away frequently or like to be able to do things on impulse, your dog may find that confusing and upsetting.

- **Are you able to give a dog the exercise it needs?** All dogs, no matter what their size or breed, need regular exercise to stay physically and mentally healthy. You will need to have the time and energy every day to provide exercise and stimulation for your dog. Make sure you or a member of your household can commit to this responsibility — rain, hail or shine. On days when you can't exercise the dog yourself, you may need to pay a dog walker or send your dog to daycare so that it gets the stimulation it needs. On the upside, having to walk your dog every day will be beneficial for your health as well as that of your pet (see pages 235–236).

- **How do you feel about dog hair and other messes?** All dogs shed some hair, and some breeds shed more than others. Your dog will need to be regularly groomed, at home or by a professional, and you will have to clean up the hair it sheds on carpets, on furniture, in the car . . . If you have allergies or prefer a low-shedding breed, there are hypoallergenic-friendly dog breeds which might be more suitable, but these dogs often need professional grooming to keep their coats short and in good condition. Dogs can also be a bit mucky: they can make muddy footprints on the floor, bring in items from outside, roll in yucky things and generally get wet and dirty from time to time, so if you like your home to be immaculate you will have to train your dog carefully and clean more thoroughly.

- **Can you cope with toilet training?** Dogs need to be taught the correct and acceptable place to do their business, especially when they are puppies or newly adopted. Accidents will happen during the training process, so you need to be prepared to invest time and patience into teaching your dog appropriate habits. You will also need to be prepared to pick up poop from your property and when you are out and about.

- **Do you have the time to invest in adequate training and socialisation?** What you put into a dog is what you will get back out. Most dogs are eager to learn and keen to please their owners, but they will need to be taught basic obedience commands and acceptable behaviour. Regular socialisation with other animals, people and situations is a must, especially for puppies, who need to be taught about the world. Training takes time, consistency and commitment, but the rewards are huge.

Before bringing a dog into your life, it is important to carefully evaluate these factors to ensure that you can provide a suitable environment, sufficient time for care and exercise, and the overall commitment required for responsible dog ownership. Talk to everyone in the family or household and be realistic — if the time isn't right now, maybe there will be a point in the future when you have more time and resources and can enjoy dog ownership to the full. That is a much more responsible decision to make than taking on a dog, then needing to rehome it when things don't work out the way you had hoped.

Dogs and kids

Many people think they'd like to get a dog for their children. Maybe they are being endlessly pestered by their kids into getting a dog, or they had one when they were young and want their own family to have the same positive experience. It can work really well — there is nothing sweeter than seeing the bond between a child and their dog — but you do have to be careful. Different dogs will react to children in different ways, and while most dogs would never intentionally hurt a child, sometimes the way children act can cause problems and trigger the dog into behaving in a way it wouldn't normally, including even snapping or biting.

Kids have naturally higher-pitched voices than adults, so dogs tend to get more excited by them — dogs associate a higher pitch with excitement, or getting rewarded and therefore get excited. (Think about how you talk to them when you praise them or are trying to encourage them to play or fetch). Kids are often also noisy and fast-moving, and wave their arms around — all of which will excite a dog. All it takes is one nip and the dog gets blamed, but you have created a situation the dog should never have been in in the first place.

It's not the child's fault, but many dogs will want to engage in play when the child is not ready or confident. The child goes to grab something or pull back and the dog thinks they're playing, then they run away and of course the dog gives chase. Some parents think it's funny to have the dog chase the child, but it's not a joke — all it's done is start a problem behaviour. You, the adult, are there to set the rules and boundaries — not only for the dog, but also for the child.

It's very important that boundaries are respected on both sides. The children need to respect the dog and its need for space. A dog is a living being and not a toy or something to climb on. Kids need to be taught how to touch the dog gently and appropriately, and how to act calmly around it. The dog's food, crate or other bed should be kid-free zones, because your dog may try to resource-guard (protect and defend things it values). Kids also need to learn about dogs' body language (see pages 260–263) so they can see the warning signs if a dog is unhappy, stressed or about to bite.

Children need to be taught to be calm around the dog and move slowly around it — you can't let the kid run around screaming and expect the dog to not react. Also, while affection is lovely, you need to not allow the child to hang around the dog's neck and kiss it on the face — it's a sign of dominance and it can upset some dogs. The last thing you want is for a child to get bitten on the face.

Likewise, the dog needs to be familiarised with children and taught how it is allowed to behave around them (for example, not jumping up, chasing, nipping in play, etc.). Parents and children can get upset when the dog chews their toys and clothes, but how is the dog to know what's theirs and what isn't? You have to teach both the dog and the children — and it's probably a good idea to keep the kids' bedroom doors closed, especially if you have a puppy.

Never leave a child alone with a dog — even if you know them both, you can't be sure how either of them will behave. The child might do something unexpected and you don't know how the dog is going to react.

I get upset when I see children in videos engaged in what is supposed to be play but is basically teasing the dog. Everyone thinks if the dog is wagging its tail then it's happy, but that's not always the case. If its ears are back, or it's licking its lips or showing the whites of its eyes ('whale eye'), these are all signs of stress, communicating that the dog is really uncomfortable or nervous (see page 261). Parents need to step in and stop this behaviour, rather than treat it as funny and encourage it.

Everyone in the household needs to be consistent and give the dog clear messages. If parents enforce the rules but the kids ignore them (or vice versa), the dog will simply get confused. Some people think I'm too strict with my dogs, but they need to know what is allowed and what isn't — and you are the one who sets the rules for your dog.

Narla, a Staffy, was adopted in mid-2020 by Sarah and her husband, Anthony, who has some experience of dog rescue: he is Helen and Gavin's son.

Sarah: We were travelling in South America in early 2020 when we saw that Helen had posted a picture of this litter, and I thought, 'Ooh, I want that puppy.' When we had to come back to New Zealand because of Covid, we were living with Anthony's parents and I helped look after Narla's litter. There was an immediate connection: when I'd go in with the puppies, she'd climb straight into my lap and not move the whole time.

We had been planning to get a dog, but not straight away — Anthony said we had to get a house before we got a dog. Narla had originally been adopted by another family, but they brought her back after twelve hours because their other, older dog didn't get on with her. I was looking at Gavin and he was looking at me and saying, 'Come on, Sarah, this is fate.' But again Anthony said no, so she got offered to another family. They decided not to take her, and this time we were all looking at Anthony. I was saying, 'Come on, this dog loves us — can we take her?'

She was about three months old when we finally took her home. We had been in lockdown, so I wasn't back at work, which meant I was able to have a lot of one-on-one time with her and work through all those little puppy things like toilet training.

She had been given the name Nga because all the puppies in her litter had names that started with N, but we changed her name to Narla because we thought it sounded better when we were calling her. She's a cool little dog but quite timid, and she usually stays pretty close to me, especially in situations she's not sure about. She's very much my dog. She's not really a chewer, and she doesn't like playing fetch: she gets the ball, but then she just looks at you like she's thinking, 'Why do you keep throwing it away?'

Not long after we got Narla, I had a serious brain injury, and having her around has been super helpful. She would have made a great therapy dog — she would come over to me and sit in my lap and get me away from feeling sorry for myself.

Around the time we got her, we were thinking about starting a family. Now we have a toddler, but she mostly avoids him. If he comes over to her, she'll get up and move away, without making a fuss.

We ended up getting a second dog because we wanted her to have a mate when our son was born, so she wouldn't be quite as put out by the change. We also thought it would be good for her to have a friend for when we went out. She's another rescue, a terrier–papillon cross called Sky. The two dogs get on really well.

I think rescue dogs just have a little bit more personality. They might come with more baggage, but who doesn't? They become part of the family, with their own little issues and things that make them special and interesting.

There is such a surplus of dogs, it seems silly to pay stupid money to a breeder for a dog that looks slightly different to or even the same as a rescue. I also feel like Narla is more grateful to have us around, having had a rough start to life. She is such a cool dog — everybody who meets her loves her.

Helen says:

Narla was one of a litter of five puppies abandoned little more than a week after New Zealand went into its first Covid lockdown in March 2020. Found huddled together in a worn-out box, these puppies faced an uphill

battle from the start, their tiny bodies infested with fleas and burdened by intestinal worms. Collaborating with another rescue, we took on the responsibility of caring for the puppies, all of which required specialised attention, drawing us closer to their unique needs and challenges.

Narla's first new home was short-lived: the family who had taken her returned her almost immediately, unable to handle their existing dog's aggression towards her. It was a tough decision for them, but even more difficult for Narla, as she had to endure yet another upheaval. Fortunately, when Sarah learned of the pup's return, she was filled with a renewed determination to adopt her and make her part of her family.

2

Why get a rescue dog?

If you have considered all the factors and decided the time is right for you to get a dog, the next question is: where are you going to get it from? Of course, we would suggest a rescue or animal shelter, where there are dogs that desperately need homes. There are already so many dogs in the world, so it makes sense to us to take in a rescue dog, rather than go to a registered breeder or, worse, get a dog from a backyard breeder or a 'puppy mill', where animals might be being kept in unhealthy or unkind conditions, kept in cages and discarded if they are no use for breeding.

A reputable rescue organisation can provide guidance and assistance in finding a dog that matches your personality, lifestyle and specific needs, and help you deal with any issues that arise. At Country Retreat, we specialise in rehoming mother dogs and their puppies. We put a lot of time and effort into taking care of the dogs and working with them to get them to a place where they can be adopted, and we want the match to work as much as you do!

If you adopt a very young rescue puppy, especially from an experienced rescue like ours, it should be like adopting any puppy, without any innate behavioural problems from past trauma, and you can train it and mould it as it grows up. Adopting an older puppy or adult dog that has been exposed to abuse, malnutrition or abandonment may mean it has some habits and anxieties which will have to be worked through. Nevertheless, in our experience it is these dogs that seem to have the most love to give. While they may have been hurt or mistreated in the past, many of them still crave love and affection and human connection, and respond so well to kindness and living in a safe, happy home where they have their needs met.

Ralph was a five-month-old huntaway–Rottweiler cross who came to our sanctuary. He had bruising over 95 per cent of his body and was losing sight in one eye from being mistreated. His original owner was going to kill him, but a visitor to the property took him away and brought him to us. When we first got him, he couldn't even sit down because of his injuries. But he is such a lovely puppy, so gentle and calm — a great example of how much love a dog can give even after being through absolute hell. He will play with the other dogs, but mostly just wants to be with people and snuggle with them. Fortunately, he didn't lose his injured eye, although it is cloudy and he has reduced vision in it, and he will make someone the most wonderful pet when he is ready to be adopted.

Another benefit of getting a rescue dog is that, while there will be an adoption fee to pay, and all the other usual expenses of having a dog (see pages 41–43), it will be a lot cheaper than buying a pure-bred puppy or designer cross-breed. Since Covid especially, prices have risen off the scale — you might be looking at paying $2000 or more even for an unpapered puppy, and still more for a pedigree dog.

In recent years a lot of people have paid outrageous prices for pure-breds and designer cross-breeds, and that's driven a lot of backyard breeders. And when backyard breeders can't sell them, they often just dump them. So while we used to get a lot of Staffy or Labrador crosses at the sanctuary, now we are getting quite a few other breeds coming through, including more desirable and fashionable breeds.

But people don't only want a rescue dog to save money upfront. Often it's because they want to do good, and give a dog in need the chance of a happy life. We have to be careful, because some people have massive hearts and want to take on a dog with issues or special needs, but don't realise the time and effort that's going to be involved. It's a balancing act trying to find out how much time people have, what they want to do with their dog and how experienced they are as an owner.

Rescue dog . . . or pure-bred?

If you are weighing up the pros and cons of a rescue dog versus a pure-bred dog or 'designer' blend, here are some other factors to consider.

- **Uniqueness:** Most rescue dogs are cross-breeds, and often without a DNA test (yes, you can get your dog's DNA tested) it's impossible to tell which breeds are in the mix. Their size, appearance and temperament may not be fully known until they mature, and can vary even within a litter of puppies — we've had litters here where the size range of the dogs once they were adults was huge. This can be part of the charm and adventure of adopting a rescue dog. Some people are looking for a specific breed because of how it looks, and can't be budged on that, but if you are prepared to be more flexible, then you may be surprised at what you can find in a rescue dog.

- **Unpredictability:** Some people also want specific breeds because of their perceived behavioural characteristics or personality, but those are not always guaranteed, even in a pure-bred dog. Each dog is a unique individual, with its own traits and quirks. And while pure-breds generally have more predictable physical and behavioural traits, they may also be prone to certain breed-specific health issues. It's important to choose a reputable breeder if opting for a pure-bred, and to look into health issues associated with that breed. With a cross-breed, especially one of unknown parentage, it's a bit more of a lottery as to what traits might turn up. Adopting a rescue dog is an ongoing adventure!

- **Background:** Rescue dogs may have a history that impacts their behaviour and needs. You may never know what the dog has experienced before its time at the rescue centre or pound. All dogs that are rehomed will have their quirks, and especially those that have had traumatic lives and been hurt or abandoned. (At Country Retreat, while it's generally easy for us to find homes for puppies, it can be harder to rehome adult dogs, especially those that may have developed behavioural problems from being mistreated.) However, some rescues, especially nowadays, will be loved family pets that have had good lives but now need a new home due to changes in their owners' circumstances. Just because a dog is a rescue doesn't mean it's going to be aggressive or have major behavioural issues. All dogs need training and consistent boundaries.

- **Gratitude:** It seems funny to say it, but many rescue dogs seem to know that they have been given a second chance at life and seem extra-grateful for the love and care you give them. Dogs are naturally a pack animal and feel happiest when they are with their special humans. If they have had a period of being abandoned or mistreated, the love you are able to give them now is extra special.

Rescue dogs: the nitty-gritty

There are lots of ways dogs end up being in need of rescue, none of them good. And by rescue, I mean these dogs are looking for homes because they have reached the end of the line. Usually they have been found abandoned and either taken to the council shelter, in line to be put to sleep if their owner can't be found, or have been taken on by a volunteer rescue operation. Sometimes a dog will have been surrendered by its owners to the SPCA or an animal shelter because they can't look after it any more due to a change in circumstances or financial pressures, or the dog's behaviour has become too hard to deal with, especially if it is aggressive or it has bitten someone. Litters of puppies get dumped, sometimes in out-of-the-way places where the chance of finding them alive is slim. They get left in rubbish bins, or people throw them in rivers and lakes, trying to drown them. Some are simply shot dead.

While we specialise in taking pregnant dogs and puppies at Country Retreat, we do end up taking on all sorts of dogs. We can help the mama dogs through their pregnancies, then make sure they are desexed, preventing the cycle of more and more unwanted puppies being born. We also make sure all the puppies that we rehome are desexed once they are old enough — that's one of the very clear conditions of getting a dog from us.

Since Covid, there has been a huge increase in the number of unwanted dogs that have needed rehoming. It's really sad to see. When the pandemic first hit, lots of people wanted to get a dog. Because of restrictions, or because people didn't understand how important it was, a lot of these dogs didn't get desexed, so when they came into season they wanted to go out and make babies. One lady we helped had a Rottweiler that the vet had refused to desex because it wasn't a year old, but at six months of age the dog came on heat. They had it fenced in, in a pen, in a kennel, but they went out shopping one day and the dog next door ate through the metal fence to get to her. They ended up with fourteen puppies, of which we ended up with ten. One, Rockie, was rehomed on the TV show (you can read his story on page 83–87). Sadly, the mother dog was ruined physically and mentally from the stress of having so many puppies at just nine months old.

The other problem generated by Covid is that a lot of dogs didn't get properly socialised over lockdown, because they weren't able to get out and about when they were puppies. There are plenty of dogs out there who didn't learn appropriate social skills, so are an absolute nightmare behaviourally, and owners are just wanting to get rid of them. Also, now that many people are no longer working from home following the relaxation of pandemic restrictions, their dogs have become lonely and bored and destructive.

When we first started the rescue operation, in 2019, we used to take only pregnant dogs and puppies. We would usually be able to get homes for all of the puppies within about three weeks, and have people on a wait list for the next litter. Now we have dogs that have been here for months and months and no one is interested in adopting them. Far fewer people can afford to take on a dog at the moment; and with the cost of living having risen, many families have to think about feeding themselves before they can even think of feeding a dog.

When people come to us to say they're going to have to surrender their dog because they can't afford to feed it, we will try to help by giving them dog food. We'd rather see the dog stay with a loving family. We also take dog food to a local hub, and they pass it on to people who are getting a human food parcel. In tough times, animals can get hungry as well, and when dogs are hungry they start wandering and scavenging and run the risk of being impounded. Pregnant females in particular may start roaming, looking for extra food. In some areas — the Far North, for instance — stray dogs are beginning to form into packs, which can be intimidating for members of the public who encounter them on the road or on a forest trail.

When a new dog comes into the sanctuary, I don't let just anyone in with it. Often we don't know anything about the dog's past, where it might have come from and how it has ended up being abandoned or surrendered. From watching it carefully, I'll try to work out what's happened in its past to cause it to be scared or reactive. For example, if a dog looks away when you offer it food, it may be because it has been hit in the past when being fed. It is now too scared to look at you in case you see it as a challenge and hurt it. In these cases, you have to take time to see how the dog reacts to people and to being approached.

If a dog's not used to being touched, or it associates being touched with pain, trying to touch it can make it uncomfortable, and that means someone might get hurt. With some dogs, you have to earn their trust before even trying to get near them. We've sat for hours outside a pen while a dog has been growling and snarling at us. We have to try to not to show our nerves, to show the dog that it doesn't intimidate us, and that we mean it no harm. Only then can we slowly start to approach and handle it.

On *The Dog House NZ*, one episode featured a beautiful German shepherd cross who was so scared, we couldn't get near her for about three weeks. She had been broken by her life experiences, but we slowly put her back together. She was adopted by experienced owners — people with enormous empathy who knew how to handle her — and now she is so happy and confident.

We also get dogs who have never really had the opportunity to *be* dogs — to play, to have the freedom to run around. It can be quite hard at the start, because you can't begin to retrain and resocialise a dog if it won't come anywhere near you. You have to work on building that trust first.

That's what a lot of people don't realise: rescue is not easy. It's not all puppy dogs and cuddles! Luckily we've only had a few dogs that have had to be put to sleep because of aggression — we can't in all conscience rehome a dog that's going to hurt somebody or hurt other animals. It's very hard, but that's the reality of rescue: it doesn't always have a happy ending. We're lucky that we can spend time with these dogs and try to help them. Often they can be turned around, but it takes time and patience. Sometimes a dog will only tolerate being handled by one specific person, and may take a long time to put its trust in anyone else. Some dogs are afraid of men, for example, so only female volunteers can handle them and Gavin has to stay away.

One of the reasons we specialise in rehoming puppies is that, although they may have had a rough start to life — being abandoned, say, or not given adequate food or medical care — they usually still have their positive puppy personalities and haven't developed behavioural issues, such as reactivity or aggression. With lots of time and love they usually grow up to be happy, loving and confident dogs.

Pace

Our longest-ever resident was Pace, a three-legged cross-breed that we really struggled to find a home for, due to her particular needs. She came to us from another rescue centre after being surrendered by her original owners. She had been kept full-time in a crate, and when she first arrived she was so fear-aggressive she wouldn't let Gavin go near her. She was also terrified of people in high-vis vests — if you had her out in the car and drove past some workmen, she would turn into a snarling Tasmanian devil! She was very nervous with people she didn't know and took a while to trust them, and preferred to be in a familiar place. But when you got to know her and she trusted you, she was a great snuggler, and I knew that if I could find the right place for her, she would be a wonderful dog.

I didn't want to give up on her, but after two-and-a-half years with us I was afraid she was becoming institutionalised, and that she would not adapt to living in the real world. She had a really nice life with us and enjoyed being with the other dogs, but I knew she would be happiest if she had a home of her own. I also knew she wouldn't be happy living in suburbia, with its many unknown and potentially frightening triggers, so I really wanted her to go to a rural property.

Fortunately, one of our volunteers, Steve, wanted to adopt her. They were living in town, so they sold their house and moved to the countryside so they could give Pace a home. It's funny: Steve hadn't liked dogs that much, but now he has three! We have certainly converted him.

It was really bittersweet when Pace left us to go and live with Steve and his family, but he still brings her back regularly, and we are always pleased to see her. She has settled in well in her new home, where she is getting the love she deserves — an amazing outcome for a dog that was one of the hardest ones we have had to rehome.

What you also need to bear in mind is that, as well as potentially having behavioural issues, sometimes rescue dogs have medical issues. A dog might have allergies and need an injection once a month to keep its skin problems under control. If you want to take that dog on, you will need to be sure you can cover that cost as well. Of course, if you get a puppy from a breeder, you don't know what health problems it might encounter later in life, so in some ways it is good to know upfront what those issues are.

I tend to take on quite a few elderly and special-needs dogs, including a few deaf dogs, which usually have medical issues, because I can see how much extra TLC they need. Some of them get rehomed — but if the older dogs end up living out their days quietly and happily with us, I'm OK with that.

The other thing many people don't realise about rescue is the scale of the need for it. On some days we might be offered twenty or thirty dogs in need of rescue. We can only take so many, as spaces become available only when other dogs are adopted, and so most of the others may be put to sleep, or

dumped to become someone else's problem. That's the really hard part for me: the ones I can't help. People say I should focus on the ones I can help, but it still breaks my heart.

I guess the answer to the question 'why get a rescue dog?' is that these animals need you. They need a forever home where someone will love and take care of them for the rest of their lives. The alternative, quite simply, is usually that they will be put down, if they are in an animal shelter. Even a rescue like ours can't afford to keep dogs forever — we need to find homes for them.

Rescue owners

What you may have seen on the TV show *The Dog House NZ* is really only a snapshot of what we do. Although it shows the usual process — a potential owner talking about what they want in a dog, then being paired with a potential match — the timeline was compressed for TV, so you don't get to see all the behind-the-scenes work that goes on to check out every featured owner. A lot of boxes need to be ticked before I am happy to let one of our dogs go home with a new owner, and I've had to vet all those potential new owners before they were even accepted to appear in the programme.

When we were filming the show, every morning we'd get up at 5 a.m. to exercise the dogs we were taking with us. While about half the show was filmed at Country Retreat, showing us working with the dogs and the sanctuary operation, the owner introductions and the meet-and-greets we shot at a studio. We knew which potential owners were going to be there each day and which dogs we thought might be a match for them, but we'd always take extras along with us.

We get a huge range of people who come to us wanting to adopt a dog — everything from young couples who've just moved into an apartment or are just starting out in life, right up to older people who are in retirement homes, and everything in between. There is not one specific type of person, and all of them want different things in a dog. Younger people tend to want dogs they can go walking and exploring with, while older people often want something small and cuddly. I'm generally quite firm about not letting older owners adopt a puppy, as it will usually be too much for them, and we also have to consider what might happen to the dog if something happens to the owner. Usually I try to talk to a family member to remind them that if anything happens to the older person, the dog is going to need to be cared for. It can be a bit upsetting to think and talk about, but we have to be open and honest. It might seem a bit ruthless, but I want the dogs to go to a forever home.

Matching a dog with an owner is often not so much to do with breeds or looks but more much to do with personalities — of both the human and the canine! A potential owner may think they want one kind of dog, but come away with something that's completely different, yet is much more suited to them and their lifestyle. What people say they want and what we believe is actually a good match for them can be quite different. Perhaps around 80 per cent of people end up with a different dog to what they expected to get. We can make the introduction, but it's often the dogs that choose the people.

We see people who come in and get so fixated on a specific dog that they don't see what's around them. That's when sometimes I have to say, 'Look behind you, there's one sitting right there. Why don't you look at that one?' You can't tell them which one to take, but you can try to help them understand what may work better for them. It's best if people come with an open mind; I am quite happy to advise them on what would work best.

Some people just want a specific-looking dog. We can have some super-cute mixed-breed puppies up for adoption and get no applications, but put up a retradoodle and we're snowed under! (And a lot of those applicants will have no idea how much grooming it will need . . .)

There are definitely some dogs I won't let go to some people. I wouldn't let a first-time dog owner go home with a Rottweiler cross or a pittie cross, or even sometimes a collie or a Staffy — they're like the Energizer bunny! People may have to accept that they're not capable of taking on certain dogs; for example, if someone is very gentle-natured and we can see the dog is going to rule the roost, we will encourage them to think again.

I pride myself on making good matches, and put a lot of time and thought into them. Since we've been running Country Retreat I've found

homes for more than 700 dogs. Only about 15 have been returned because the match didn't work out — and all of those have subsequently been rehomed. It's important to note that none of the returns have been through any fault of the dog. One of the hardest things I've learned is that people lie, and that really hurts me. I want the best for the dogs, and I've worked so hard to get these dogs to the point where they can go out into their new homes, so when people aren't honest about their circumstances or lifestyle, and whether or not they can actually look after a dog properly, it's just a waste of everybody's time. Our contract says we have first option if the dog is to be returned, but unfortunately we can't always just take them back if someone changes their mind or finds they can't handle it after all — we just don't have the space.

I like matching people with dogs — it gives me satisfaction to not only find a happy home for the dog but also to make someone's life better, in the special way that having a dog can. I love it when people send photos of the dogs they got through us, sharing their new lives and saying how much they love their dog. There are some days when I feel we're just not doing enough to help all the needy dogs out there, so when I see a photo of a dog that was once in a bad situation and is now living a happy life and being loved, it makes me feel a lot better. This book includes stories about some of the wonderful people who have adopted dogs from us over the past few years and the difference it has made to their lives.

The adoption process

One of the big things about our rescue operation is that no one else does the rehoming and makes the decisions about which dog goes with which owner — that side of the sanctuary just stops if I'm busy. I don't want anyone else to have the responsibility of putting a dog into the wrong place. It's down to me if it doesn't work out. I started the sanctuary, I've built it up, and I take my responsibilities very seriously.

Before I even let people come up to the sanctuary and start meeting dogs, there's some basic paperwork required. They need to fill out an adoption application form, which asks for information about their property, family members and other pets. I do all the checking first, so we're not wasting anybody's time — or getting any doggy hopes up! A lot of people take one look at the form and give up, but that's a good way to weed people out. It's part of the test, to have to go through these little hurdles. If you can't be bothered to complete the form, are you really serious about taking care of a dog for fifteen years? Even if everything looks good on paper, it's still not guaranteed that they will get a dog, but the chances are more likely.

I need to see photos or a video of their section and how it is fenced, and where the dog is going to be kept when they're out. One of our stipulations is that the property the dog is going to live on has to be fully fenced, so the dog can't escape and go wandering. Of course, a lot of people who come to us are rural, and they're not going to be able to put a suburban-style fence around several hectares. In cases like these, we need to see an area where the dog will be safe and secure when they are not on the property. It could be a deck with shade from the sun or a large pen where they have space to move around — not a run, where they are tied or chained. I absolutely will not let one of our dogs be chained — I will remove the dog if I find out it is being left tied up. Some people will try to tell me that they don't need a pen because the dog is never left alone, but I insist that there is a safe, secure area for the dog. Everyone goes out sometimes!

In the suburbs, I require potential owners to have at least a completely enclosed back section, with adequate-height fences: some dogs can be real Houdinis and jump very high! Also, we want our dogs to sleep inside — they're not outside working dogs. I'm not against that in appropriate situations, but our dogs are to be family members, and they need to be in the house with you when you're home, not sitting outside by themselves.

If the initial checks look good, I invite applicants to come to the sanctuary and meet some dogs. As soon as people arrive at Country Retreat, they're being assessed. I'm watching all the time how they act, how they interact with the dogs, what they say. If I'm unsure about introducing them to a potential adoption, I'll bring in our dogs first to see how they react. Everyone thinks I'm their best friend, but I'm doing that for a reason — I need to make them feel really at ease, so things will slip out — and if I don't think it's going to work out, I'll say so. The dogs are my priority — I'm not here to make friends!

I do let people who are renting adopt dogs, otherwise the pool of potential owners would be greatly reduced. It's hard, though, because there are more restrictions and the owners have less control over where they might be living and what environment they can provide for their dog. I always make sure they have their current landlord's permission to get a dog, but that doesn't mean that they're not going to move out or need somewhere else to live in the future.

We charge a nominal fee for each adoption ($365, as at late 2023). For that money, you are getting a dog with all the 'set-up costs' paid for: initial vaccinations, desexing, microchipping and registration, which done separately would cost around $500 or more. It's not about the money, though. As well as going towards covering our costs, the reason that we put a fee on adoption is also because we feel it gives the dog more value in people's minds. It's not something they've just got for free — easy come, easy go. It's like if you have a question, you're going to put more store in the answer you get from a solicitor whom you're paying by the hour (or the minute) than from someone on the street. If you haven't paid for the dog, how much are you going to value it?

The fee helps to set a bar of sorts: if you're not able to come up with this fee upfront, and are therefore likely to struggle to pay for food and vet care, ultimately it's the dog that suffers. It also helps to weed out tyre-kickers, my pet hate. I work seven days a week and don't have any time to waste — especially on people who have no intention of adopting a dog, but just want to look at the puppies!

Other dogs

If a potential owner already has other dogs, we need them to be both desexed and fully vaccinated. I also invite them to bring their other dog with them to meet their potential fur-sibling, as the best way to see the dynamic between the dogs is to introduce them away from their own territory. Their current dog is at a disadvantage, in a completely new place with lots going on and lots of other animals, so I can get an understanding of what that dog is like when it's out of its comfort zone.

We do the first introduction with both dogs on leads. Because dogs can sense their owners' emotional states, and anxiety can be transmitted down the lead to the dog, we can take it out of the owners' hands if we think they're going to be nervous and cause a problem. One of the more experienced volunteers, or Gavin or I, will do that. If the owner is confident enough, they can hold their own dog. Once the dogs have had a good sniff, and if they seem to be compatible, then we let them play freely and I observe how they get on.

As much as possible we try to do the first introduction here, especially with adult dogs. With puppies it's totally different, as there are not many adult dogs that would attack a puppy — they're just going to tell them off, because puppies are annoying! In those cases we usually let the new owners take the puppy home and do the introductions there.

Michelle adopted Leo the Rottweiler–huntaway cross in 2022, after falling in love with him while volunteering at Country Retreat. He is now part of the family, living with Michelle and her daughter Holly, eight-year-old Border collie Rusty and a ragdoll cat on an 8-acre section near Matakana.

We've usually always had two dogs, but at the time we met Leo we had just the one Border collie, Rusty. My daughter, Holly, and I had been volunteering at the sanctuary with the puppies, and one day Gavin came in with this four-month-old puppy that was being picked on in his pen by the other dogs. He had a scratch on his head and was a very sad-looking little boy — very 'woe is me'.

I picked him up and gave him a cuddle and he stayed in my arms for about twenty minutes, resting his head on my shoulder. I fell in love . . . and next minute, Gavin was putting a 20 kg bag of puppy food in the back of my car and Rockie (as he was then) was coming home with us, just for the weekend, to have a break. He never went back! We renamed him Leo because we thought having a Rusty and a Rockie was a bit much.

He fitted in really well. He's a really placid, chilled dog, fine with the cat, doesn't chase the chickens. He's just an easy, relaxed guy who does his own thing. He can also be very social — when we take him to the beach, he's like, 'Where are the dogs? I'm off.'

The two dogs get on great and keep each other company. Leo is going to keep Rusty young. They run and chase each other at the beach. The Border collie always has to find a stick, then Leo comes along and steals it. He doesn't want the stick — he wants Rusty to chase him. He runs off, looking back cheekily over his shoulder to see if Rusty is coming after him. It's nice that they're buddies so that if we go out, they go somewhere together and hang out.

We had to do some training with him, but he's really good at taking cues from the Border collie. I can walk him around the streets here off the leash — I just tell him to wait if needs be.

Like any dog he's a big lover of cat food. We have a big white fluffy ragdoll, and when the dogs are sitting in the sun, the cat rubs up against them and puts his tail in their faces, but they're just not bothered.

Having a dog completely changes your life. I could never be without one now. Our two have basically become our best friends, and when they're not here the house feels so wrong. When we got back from holiday recently, we weren't supposed to pick them up for another day, but I said, 'that's it, we're going to get the dogs' — the house was too quiet without them. They're well and truly part of our family, and I love that.

I think Helen and Gavin do amazing work — they are the most giving people you could ever meet. I don't know how they do it. Helping them was a motivation for adopting Leo, as it gives back a little bit.

It's nice to give a home to a dog that's not been cared about. All of them have had such terrible circumstances placed upon them, but they don't have any say. I could easily end up with ten dogs and fall in love with all of them. When you take the big ones up the drive and along the road for a walk, you can see how happy you make them. Volunteering at the sanctuary is good for the soul: you can forget about what's going on in your life and just be with them, giving them some of the love that they deserve, and it fills your bucket.

Helen says:

The local animal shelter called to see if we could help, as a very young pup had been dropped off. It was only about six weeks old— way too young to be away from the mummy dog, so they had done a good job of keeping this pup alive and healthy. The reason this puppy had been dropped at the pound was so sad for the family, who loved him. Unfortunately they had found out their youngest child was highly allergic to dogs — so much so that he ended up very sick in hospital. Once the family knew the pup was the source of their child's allergic reaction they had no option but to rehome the dog as quickly as possible.

    He was an absolute delight, so full of life and energy. We integrated him into another litter of pups who were approximately the same age, and he flourished.

    Leo (then named Rockie) appeared on the TV show *The Dog House NZ*, but unfortunately he wasn't adopted then, as the prospective family was concerned about how big he might grow. Fortunately, Michelle and Holly fell in love with him. This family had been through a very hard few years, and I believe Leo was instrumental in helping them deal with the heartbreak they had recently suffered. I remember Michelle saying they had forgotten how to smile and laugh, and little Leo brought so much joy back into their lives.

3

What sort of dog should you get?

Many people have an idea in their head of what their 'ideal' dog would be like, or have their heart set on a particular breed. But as far as I'm concerned, when it comes to making matches between owners and dogs, personality and lifestyle compatibility count for more than whether a dog has the right 'look' or is a certain breed. All dogs are worthy of love, and the dog that is most drawn to you, and vice versa, might surprise you.

At the sanctuary, once I've talked to would-be owners, and seen how they and their children or teens behave around the dogs, I will have a good idea of what would suit them. Even if they think they know what they want, I'll sometimes say, 'I think you should have a look at this dog.' I can't always change people's minds, but I can put other dogs out there as options.

There are some general factors to consider when thinking about what sort of dog might fit best into your family and home. Here are some of the major ones.

- **Lifestyle:** Are you an active person who wants a dog to accompany you on lots of adventures and exercise with you? Or do you spend a lot of time around the home and are looking for a companion for cuddles? Different breeds have different exercise needs and energy levels, so if you're an active person with the time and energy to keep up with a high-energy dog, a small, lively breed like a terrier or a working dog like a Border collie — one of New Zealand's favourite dogs — might be a great fit. Conversely, if you prefer a more relaxed and low-key lifestyle, a larger, calmer dog might be a better choice. Don't be fooled into thinking that smaller dogs are always easier to manage than large dogs! Temperament plays a significant role in a dog's behaviour and energy level, regardless of size. Small terriers and other high-energy breeds can seem to have everlasting batteries, demanding plenty of mental and physical stimulation. On the other hand, larger dogs, especially some mastiff breeds, can have a more relaxed and laid-back temperament, and may be content with shorter walks and more downtime. However, it's important to note that all dogs require proper socialisation and regular exercise to ensure their health and well-being. There's no such thing as a dog that doesn't need to be walked. The key is to match the dog's temperament and energy level to your own lifestyle and capabilities.

- **Size:** Do you want a small, large or medium-sized dog? Think about the size of your home and property: is there plenty of space for a large dog to move around comfortably inside and out, or is it better suited to something more compact? How big is your garden or outdoor area? Do you want to be able to pick up and carry your dog when necessary? What size of dog will fit in your car? As we mentioned above, the size of the dog may not have an impact on its temperament: some small dogs have big-dog personalities, and big dogs might be big wusses, so think more about practical considerations here. A bigger dog will also cost more to feed, and some vet bills may be higher — desexing costs are based on weight, and if your dog needs other procedures such as surgery there may be a higher cost for anaesthetics.

- **Your age and capabilities:** If you're older or have physical limitations, a smaller or lower-energy breed will be more manageable. Also, are there any children in the household, and how old are they? Some dogs are definitely better with children than others, although again that will come down to personality as well as breed. You might like to consider getting a smaller dog that younger children will be able to walk and play with safely — or get something bigger if you have a teenager who needs to work off some energy!

- **Time:** How much time can you spend with the dog, exercising and stimulating it? If you have limited time for daily exercise and play, it's best to opt for dog with lower energy needs, or be prepared to pay out for daycare or a dog walker. Some dogs are also more temperamentally suited to being left alone while you are at work, while others suffer from terrible separation anxiety, although again that is often more related to personality than breed.

- **Previous experience with dogs:** Some breeds can be more challenging for first-time dog owners, due to their independent and strong-willed nature, while others are known for being easy-going and easy to train. It's one of the reasons Labradors and retrievers are so popular! Again, this will come down to the personality of the dog, but certain breeds are more likely to be laid-back and others more of a challenge.

- **Other pets:** Do you already have other pets, or other dogs? Some breeds and breed mixes (Labradors and retrievers again) are known for being better with other animals, while terrier-type dogs and those with a high prey drive may struggle to live peacefully with cats and other small animals. If you already have another dog you will need to consider whether they will get on (see pages 103–105), and just because they are the same breed this is not guaranteed.

New Zealand's favourite breeds

New Zealand is a nation of dog lovers, and while there are a wide range of breeds represented here, some breeds are more popular than others. Different types tend to go through phases of being in fashion, while others have been popular for years. 'Designer dogs' — cross-breeds such as spoodles, cavoodles and labradoodles — and toy dogs such as French bulldogs and pugs seem to be the thing at the moment. In general, however, the following are the dog breeds most favoured by Kiwis.

- **Labrador:** Labs are cheerful, easy-going and great with kids, although they aren't always that bright — they think everyone should love them so they can be a bit full-on. They need quite a lot of exercise, too, as they are usually very food-focused (we call them a 'stomach on legs') and can easily get a bit fat.

- **Retriever:** A retriever would be our top pick for a first-time owner looking for a great family dog.

- **Border collie:** These dogs are highly intelligent, active and friendly, with a strong herding instinct. They need *lots* of stimulation and interaction, but are great companions.

- **Huntaway/heading dogs:** Due to the number of farm dogs in New Zealand, these breeds are usually near the top of the list of dog registrations. The huntaway is a New Zealand breed, created by crossing several different sheepdog breeds, including the Border collie, Labrador and Rottweiler. Because they have been bred to move animals with their voice, they can tend to bark a lot when excited, and it's a big, deep bark, too.

- 🐾 **Jack Russell:** These little dogs are super-cute balls of energy. Originally bred to chase rats, they come in smooth and rough-coated varieties and are great for active families.

- 🐾 **Staffordshire bull terrier (Staffy):** While some people find these dogs intimidating to look at, Staffies are lovable goofballs who can be real softies. While they are only a medium-size dog, they are all muscle. A lot of rescue dogs seem to have a bit of Staffy in them.

- 🐾 **German shepherd / Alsatian:** Used around the world as police or guard dogs, German shepherds might look intimidating, but are intelligent and loyal, and respond well to training.

- 🐾 **Miniature schnauzer:** These little dogs are popular because of their cute looks and hypoallergenic coats. They do, however, need regular grooming and clipping.

- 🐾 **Chihuahua:** Well suited to urban living and smaller properties, chihuahuas may look tiny but can have big personalities. If well socialised and trained, they can make lovely, loyal companions, especially for people who aren't able to be active.

- 🐾 **Mixed breeds:** A huge number of dogs in New Zealand are 'specials' or 'fruit salads' — dogs with a bit of several breeds in them. Rescue dogs are often made up of a combination of different breeds — and with litters of puppies of unknown parentage, only time will tell which physical and personality characteristics will come through. They can be quite hardy compared to some pure-bred dogs — where faults are often intensified through close breeding — and they will often display the best aspects of several breeds.

Other popular breeds include spaniels like the cavalier King Charles and cocker spaniels; poodles and poodle crosses; toy dogs like the shih tzu, bichon frisé or Maltese; and fox terriers and Rottweilers.

Adult dog or puppy?

Everyone loves puppies, but they are a lot of work. It is like having a baby, although even babies don't usually pee and poop on the carpet at inconvenient times! We specialise in pregnant mums and puppies at Country Retreat because we see them as being the most vulnerable: they are the most likely to be put down at the pound, especially the mothers, because it's cheaper to put down one pregnant dog than her whole litter, which is so sad. Puppies need a lot of care and attention, and often the staff at council shelter facilities just don't have the time to put into them, and they don't thrive.

If we have rescued a pregnant mother and the pups are born at the sanctuary, we know we can give them a great start in life, and the pups will have known nothing but loving care all their lives. Unfortunately, puppies that we have rescued after birth, either with their mother or without (if only the litter has been abandoned), may have experienced cruelty in their young lives, and it takes us a bit more work to nurse these pups back to health and out of a state of malnutrition.

So if you want to take on a puppy, you will need to put in a lot of time and effort. I recommend that someone is at home with the puppy the majority of the time for the first six months — you can't leave it at home alone and go back to work without expecting to come back to a house that has been destroyed! You will need to give it lots of positive attention, socialising and training, including toilet training (see page 244). Puppies will be puppies, and they will chew things they shouldn't, eat stuff that isn't good for them, make messes in the wrong place, not listen to or understand instructions, and generally be pretty frustrating! But they are so cute, it is hard to stay mad at them, even if they steal your socks and chew your TV remote. From day one of taking that puppy home, you need to teach it the boundaries and guide it in a positive way to becoming an awesome dog. In return, the puppy will be more settled and better behaved if it knows what it can and can't do (this applies to adult dogs as well).

Having a puppy is also hard work initially because you have to be very careful where they go and what they do until they are completely vaccinated. That said, they still need to get out and about in order to become socialised, and see and hear different things in the world, but you will have to carry them: you can't put them down or let them be in contact with unknown, possibly unvaccinated dogs. Because of the risk of parvo (see page 201) they're restricted in where they can go: on your premises, or at the homes of fully vaccinated dogs. No walking down the road, no parks, no beaches. This is such a critical learning time, but you have to be very careful that they don't pick up any nasty diseases while they are at such a vulnerable age and stage.

However, the advantage of adopting a puppy is that they are like a blank canvas, and with proper training and socialisation you will have the opportunity to shape their behaviour and personality as they grow into adulthood.

Getting an adult dog, especially a rescue or rehomed dog, means you don't have to deal with the puppy phase, but it may yet have its own challenges. You may have the advantage of knowing the dog's history and some of its behaviour traits upfront. You'll need to find out as much as you can about the dog's background and carefully assess any potential behavioural issues it may have. It may have been exposed to abuse, or simply starved of love and attention, either of which can lead to behavioural problems, ranging from anxiety and timidness through to aggression and reactivity (see page 257). We even get some adult dogs that have not been properly toilet-trained and don't have any basic manners.

Many older dogs do have the basics, though, and they are often superkeen to please and learn to fit in with your family environment, with a bit of time, support and training. Older dogs are also likely to be more settled and less endlessly energetic.

Regardless of whether you choose a puppy or an older dog, consistent rules, boundaries and training are essential for either to thrive in your home. The effort you put into training and building a strong bond with your new companion during the initial months will influence its behaviour going forward.

Male or female?

Many potential owners have set ideas about whether they want a 'boy' or 'girl' dog, expecting its gender to make a difference to its personality and behaviour. The reality is that, in desexed dogs, these factors come down to the individual dog rather than whether it is male or female. In male dogs especially, neutering makes a big difference: removing testosterone from the dog's system minimises a lot of the typical behaviours such as marking, humping, dominance behaviours and potential aggression towards other dogs — it gets rid of that bolshy side. Desexing won't change a dog's basic personality (see page 121), but it will definitely calm down the males.

Some people come along and say they want to get a female dog because they don't want a dominant dog — but again, gender makes no difference here, and you can get some pretty stroppy females! It all comes down to personality.

For us, gender doesn't matter. We currently have three female dogs and one male, and it works out just fine. Taking hormones and breeding urges out of the picture means that mixing boys and girls shouldn't be an issue.

Other dogs and other pets

Some people come to us looking for a second dog — either to find a companion for their existing dog, or because their first dog is getting old and they want there to be an overlap, rather than 'replace' that dog when it passes away. I'm OK with that if someone is an experienced owner or they've had two dogs before. It's very rare for us to approve someone getting two puppies at the same time; I'll usually suggest they take one now and come back and see us in six to eight months' time, when the intense puppy phase has passed and they will have a better idea of whether they definitely want to take on another dog.

It can be really nice to have two or more dogs, for both the owners and the dogs. (We have almost always had multiple dogs — at least two at a time — although I accept that not everyone is up to having four, like we do currently!) Dogs are pack animals, and if two get on well they can be great companions for each other, especially if their owners are out for a few hours. Even if they merely tolerate each other, they still have company.

The success of adding a second dog depends totally on the dogs concerned. It will all come down to personalities, and whether they are compatible. It's like us humans: some people are happier on their own or with their immediate family, some are selective about who they spend time with, and some people are super-social and happy to get along with anybody. Likewise, some dogs love company and are happy to live with other dogs, while some aren't that interested, and others just don't like other dogs at all — and there's nothing wrong with that as long as you know how to manage it (see page 244). People think in order to have a 'good dog' it has to love everyone and everything, but I don't reckon that's true; as long as it is not aggressive, it has the right to its own preferences. Some breeds are known for being more friendly and easy-going, but not even all Labradors like all other dogs.

Luckily, our dogs all get along, and when our kids come to visit we sometimes have up to eight dogs in the house. We did once have a grumpy, antisocial dog (Muttley), but that was just him and we worked around it, keeping him separate if there were going to be other dogs around.

People often think it would be nice to get two dogs from the same litter, but just because dogs are siblings doesn't mean they're going to like each other (like some humans!). Dogs don't really understand if the other dog is their sibling — it doesn't matter to them. They all have their own individual traits and personalities, and that will be more important than whether they had the same mother and grew up in the same household.

When introducing a new dog to your existing dog, there will need to be firm rules and boundaries around what is and what isn't allowed. They will need to be taught to respect each other's space, including food and bedding. Ensuring each pet has its own space, resources and time with you can help reduce any feelings of competition or territorial behaviour.

When introducing a new dog, it's essential to do so gradually and in a controlled environment to minimise any potential conflicts. Observing their body language and behaviour during initial interactions will give you some idea of how the dogs may get along in the long run. Some dogs will just get on straight away and form strong bonds with their new furry sibling. Others might need more time and patience to adjust to the new dynamic. Be prepared for a period of adjustment, and be willing to provide individual attention and training to ensure each pet feels secure and valued.

Dogs and cats can also happily live together if they are given time to get to know each other. We have two cats who get on fine with our four dogs. Sometimes dogs and cats end up being fast friends and snuggle buddies, or they might just tolerate each other, but you do need to take care when they are first introduced, whether it is the dog joining a cat household or vice versa.

Never leave a cat and dog alone together until you are certain that they are comfortable with each other, and be aware that some breeds of dog are more likely to be aggressive towards or chase cats, especially if they have a strong prey drive. And always make sure the cat has an escape route: somewhere it can retreat to, up high, to get away from the dog.

Puppies and older dogs

If you already have another, older dog, you need to consider if it will be able to cope with the demands of having a puppy around. Puppies have no off-switch and can often be quite annoying to older dogs, jumping on them and nipping them in play. An older dog is allowed to tell a puppy off, and the puppy needs to learn the lesson — but often it doesn't, and even when it gets a clear telling-off, it will go back again and again. If this is happening, it's the human's responsibility to step in and take the puppy away, maybe for some downtime in its crate (see pages 146–153). Alternatively, the older dog might like some crate time to get away from the puppy!

**Bond and his family adopted Stella,
from the 'Alcohol' litter (see page 112), in 2020.
In 2023 they returned to the sanctuary to
adopt papillon Yoda as a companion for her.**

I've always been around dogs, all my life. I am originally from Indonesia and my parents always had dogs.

Stella was our first rescue dog. Mumu, our husky, used to board in the kennels at Country Retreat, so we knew Helen and Gavin. When Mumu passed away, we got Yoda, so Stella would have a friend.

We could see what Helen was doing with the sanctuary and that she was putting in a lot of effort. We talked to our kids about it, and they got into the idea of getting a rescue rather than buying a dog from a breeder. We explained to them what Helen does, and said that if we were able to help in some way, we should do that.

We got Stella as a puppy — she turned out to be one of the smallest in her litter. When we got Yoda he was a bit older. He hadn't really had any training, so even though he was a year old, he would still just go to the toilet in the house. We have had to retrain him, and sometimes he still forgets.

Stella kept her original name from being part of the 'Alcohol' litter — it's short for Stella Artois — but Yoda was originally called Sebastian. The kids named him Yoda because of his big ears.

The two dogs get on well and keep each other company during the day.

Yoda likes to act like he's the boss, which is pretty funny because Stella is bigger. We take both dogs out walking on a double leash. Stella always wants to go fast and Yoda slow, so their roles change a bit. Stella is not trying to be dominant; she just loves going for a walk. She is a bit protective of Yoda, and of our youngest girl, and likes to keep an eye on them.

Like all dogs, rescues have their own personalities. A lot of them are scared of being left behind, as they might have been abandoned when they were younger. Neither of our two really likes being left alone, but at least they have each other. Mumu didn't care if we were around or not, but these two really want to be with us. They look sad when we go to work and the kids go off to school.

Stella is timid with other dogs; she's a little better with humans, but is very wary of people she doesn't know, so we have tried to socialise her. Now that she goes out with a dog walker every day and is around other dogs, she has improved, though she is still a bit nervous and will bark at new people. Yoda is very friendly — he will play with anyone.

When we got Stella we thought it would be good to have a dog house, because Mumu liked his dog house. One day we came home and the wall of it was destroyed — she'd chewed it off! We'd just bought it for her, so that wasn't great, but you have to take the bad with the good. She didn't like the dog house — she preferred to just have a bed. It's easier for us, too, because we can move it around, and take it to the bedroom when we go upstairs to bed.

Having dogs feels like having another child. It's challenging and it's fun, good and bad. When you rescue a dog, it's a commitment. Any dog that you get from a puppy is always a challenge, and that's particularly so with Stella, and yet she is the sweetest dog I have ever owned. She always wants to please us, so it's easy to train her. She doesn't need the treats — she simply wants praise and attention.

Every year when we go to Whangārei for a dance competition, we take the dogs to Country Retreat and they stay there. Stella still remembers them — she goes straight to Helen every time, like she remembers how kind she was to her.

Helen says:

We first learned of what would become known as the 'Alcohol' litter when we received a call from an owner who was desperate for help. She had thought that having puppies would be fun and cute, and that she would make some money from selling them. But it hadn't turned out that way.

Unaware of how to properly care for a pregnant dog, the owner confined the young mummy dog to a garden shed as her due date approached. Locked away and alone, this poor dog must have been frightened and confused. When the time came, she gave birth to a whopping thirteen puppies, and miraculously, they were all alive.

But as the weeks passed, the mum and her pups were left neglected and abandoned. The neighbours began to complain about the commotion coming from the shed. The owner claimed that the mother had become aggressive towards her puppies — a predictable consequence of being confined to such a small space without respite.

We agreed to step in and take the puppies, on the condition that the mother dog would be desexed once the pups reached eight weeks of age. We agreed to cover all the costs, to make sure it happened. The owner then brought us eleven of the pups, deciding to keep two for herself.

We had a lengthy discussion with the owner, providing her with puppy milk, dog food and worming tablets. We emphasised the importance of proper care for the remaining pups and the mother. She promised to keep in touch, but sadly, that was the last we heard from her. Despite our repeated attempts to reach out, there was no response.

The eleven pups arrived in a pitiful state. The round bellies that the owner mistook for being full of milk were actually swollen with worms. Three of the pups were particularly small and weak. The owner didn't know exactly how old they were, but we estimated that they were around two to three weeks old, just beginning to take their wobbly first steps.

We spent hours removing fleas and ticks from the pups, washing them and treating them for parasites. We fed them a carefully blended mixture of puppy milk, softened biscuits and special dog food designed to settle their delicate stomachs. They needed to be fed every two to three hours, in small

quantities, as their tiny bodies struggled to absorb larger meals.

Slowly but surely, the majority of the pups started responding well to our care, gaining weight and growing stronger, and we were able to find homes for all of them.

Unfortunately, the story didn't end there. Less than a year after we rescued the litter of pups, we got another phone call about a mother dog struggling to care for her newborn pups. When we arrived to collect the pups, we realised this was the same owner, with the same mother dog, facing the same challenges all over again.

This time round, we were determined not to repeat the same mistakes. We took immediate action and physically collected the mummy dog and the pups. She was brought into our care and, without hesitation, we arranged for her to be desexed, eliminating the possibility of any future litters.

4

Bringing your dog home

The adoption papers are signed, the agreement has been made with the sanctuary, the puppies are weaned and ready to leave their mum — it's time to bring your new dog home. With a bit of preparation and thinking ahead, and some clear boundaries in place, your new dog's transition to living in your home should go smoothly.

Before you arrange to bring the dog home, ensure you have all the basic necessary supplies. You will need:

- food — appropriate to the dog's age and stage
- bowls for food and water — make sure they are sturdy and can't easily be knocked over or chewed
- dog bed or crate (see page 144), with a nice soft, welcoming blanket
- pet insurance
- a few toys
- a collar and lead — although you might like to wait until you have the dog so you can try these on to ensure they fit well
- a supply of poop bags
- grooming equipment, such as a dog brush.

For the first few days, all that's really required is the basics of food, water and a bed. The most important thing is to create a calm, supportive environment so the dog feels welcomed and safe, and can start making this new place its home.

Collars

Dogs don't need to wear a collar all the time. Some people prefer for their dog not to wear a collar when it's at home, because it can get caught on things, like a loose nail on the deck or fence — our own dogs don't wear a collar when they're at home for this reason. Their collars can easily be clipped on when it's time to go for a walk. However, especially in urban situations, it can be good to leave the dog's collar on in case it gets out of your property and goes wandering. It's also useful to have a tag with the dog's name and your phone number on the collar, so anyone who comes across the dog can give you a call.

Registration and microchipping

If you have brought home an adult dog from a rescue centre or breeder, it will probably already be microchipped and registered with the appropriate local body. You will need to update the microchip information and council registration to reflect your details and the dog's new name (if you have changed it), or register the dog yourself if you have adopted a puppy. Puppies are usually microchipped at around eight weeks, at their first vaccination.

Microchipping — where a tiny computer chip, smaller than a grain of rice, is inserted under the dog's skin, usually on the back of the neck — is legally required for all dogs registered in New Zealand for the first time. Each dog is assigned a unique fifteen-digit number, which is used to help identify your dog through its registration records and the National Dog Database. If your dog is found wandering, a vet or the council can scan the chip and your

details will come up. The microchip itself usually costs around $20, plus the vet's fee for insertion, but it lasts for the lifetime of the dog.

At Country Retreat, we have all the puppies microchipped at eight weeks, and have the chip registered in my name. Our adoption contract states that the dog has to be desexed by six months of age, at which point I will transfer the microchip registration to the owner. If this condition is not met, the dog is still officially 'mine' and I will reclaim it.

Your dog will also need to be registered annually with your local council, and each year you will be issued with a tag for the dog to wear on its collar. Councils usually offer a reduced registration cost if the dog is desexed and if you complete some 'responsible dog owner' education.

You can be fined if your dog is not microchipped and/or is unregistered with your local council.

Naming your dog

Deciding on a dog's name is always fun, though it can take a while to find a name that really suits the dog and 'sticks'. You might already have a favourite name in mind, or it might take a few days for you to get to know the dog's personality and quirks and decide what name suits it. Dogs will learn their name really quickly, which is pretty cool when you think about it. They learn to respond not just to a tone of voice but to an actual word, a combination of sounds that they understand refers uniquely to them. To teach a dog or puppy its name, start out by calling it in a higher-pitched voice and rewarding it when it responds. Pretty soon, your dog will make the connection: that's me they're talking to!

The good news is that dogs are pretty adaptable, and if you start off with one name and then decide later that it's just not right, the dog will get quickly used to the alternative. Most of the dogs that are adopted from the sanctuary are given a new name by their new owners — and, of course, we might have just given them a name when they came in, if we didn't know what their original name was. We will also change their name if it has a negative association for them; if they have been called and then hit, for example.

When we have a big litter of puppies at the sanctuary it can be hard to think of names for all of them. Usually we just call them all 'Puppy' when they are little. When they are ready for adoption, we name them so that potential owners can identify and relate to them. We usually try to base the names around a theme: for example, we had a litter recently where the mother dog's name was Fiona, so we gave all the puppies names that related to the movie *Shrek*. Sometimes we use themes like flowers, drinks, gemstones or Disney characters, and so on.

To raise money for the sanctuary, we put pictures of the litters on our Facebook page and run auctions for the naming rights, according to the theme. Someone might offer $5 to name the puppy Lord Farquaad, for example, then someone else might say they'll give us $10 to name it Donkey. We just ask that no inappropriate names are suggested — although the one time I didn't do that, one of my son's friends put in a winning bid to name a puppy Nipplewort in a 'herb'-themed auction! We took his $50 and called the puppy Lapsana, which is the Latin name for the plant.

You can call your dog anything you like, but remember you're probably going to be calling it out loud at the dog park, so names that are short and easy to understand are best. You might not want to be shouting a huge, long name repeatedly at the top of your voice — unless you can come up with a short version or nickname. Most people end up talking to their dogs using a variety of nicknames and short versions at home anyway. The top names for dogs in New Zealand in 2022 were all short and sweet: Luna, Bella, Charlie, Poppy and Coco.

Desexing

As we have said earlier in the book, having your dog desexed is vitally important. Unless you are a registered breeder, there is absolutely no reason for your male or female dog to remain entire (non-desexed). We have puppies at the sanctuary desexed as soon as possible (at around six months old), to make sure they are sterilised before they reach their first heat (in the case of females) or before males reach puberty. It's the only way to be 100

per cent sure your dog isn't going to sire or give birth to an unwanted litter.

If you adopt an adult dog from a sanctuary, it should already be desexed, or there should be a contract in place to have it desexed at a set age. If you get a young puppy, this will probably be your responsibility. The cost of desexing varies, but is substantial. Your vet may be able to help out with a payment plan.

Again, having the dog desexed is one of the cast-iron conditions of adopting a dog from us. I keep files on all the puppies we find homes for, and spend hours following up to make sure all the owners go through with the operation once the dog is six months old. So far, I have had a 100 per cent hit rate, but it does take a lot of time and effort.

Desexing costs

Due to multiple factors, the cost of desexing has increased enormously — basically doubled — over the past few years. Currently it is usually around $300 for males and $600 for females. Given that desexing is non-negotiable for us, it has become a huge financial burden for the sanctuary; we really struggle with the cost of it. However, we are reluctant to increase our adoption fee in case it puts off prospective owners.

In 2021 a national desexing programme was launched to provide free or low-cost clinics around the country. It's estimated around 220,000 dogs in New Zealand — about a quarter of the total dog population — are not desexed, and cost is often a barrier. Some rescuers can help with the cost of desexing through grants.

Desexing requires surgery. In males, the dog is castrated by the surgical removal of the testicles. (The scrotum then shrivels up over time.) For female dogs, the surgery (called spaying) is slightly more complex, as it involves the removal of the internal sexual organs — the ovaries and uterus. This means a longer anaesthetic and surgery time.

Most male dogs recover from desexing within a couple of days of taking things quietly, though it may take females longer to get over the surgery. They may need to wear a head-cone to stop them licking or chewing the wound while it is healing, and be prevented from jumping or running about too much over the next week or so. This is where crate training comes in handy (see pages 146–153).

It can take a while for testosterone to work its way out of a male dog's system after the operation, especially if it isn't neutered until it is older, but the operation will often help it to calm down and make it less likely to hump other dogs and inanimate objects, mark everything with urine, be dominant with other dogs and generally be a bit too boisterous. It also stops males from wanting to escape from your property in search of fertile females — which they can smell from miles away. Desexing your male dog also eliminates the risk of testicular cancer.

Entire male dogs can get targeted by other dogs when they're out walking or at the park. Other dogs, even if they are desexed, will be able to smell the entire dog's hormones and may try to dominate him or act aggressively. Your dog might be really gentle-natured, but other dogs, male and female, might be keen to have a go at him.

For female dogs, spaying doesn't so much change their personality or behaviour: it just eliminates the risk of pregnancy. As well as male dogs seeking them out, female dogs on heat may also try to get out and find a mate, with predictable but unfortunate consequences. Being desexed also reduces the female's risk of getting mammary tumours (breast cancer). The risk of this developing increases every time the dog is in heat.

If your female dog is in heat, she will have to be kept at home, preferably inside, for two or three weeks. Trying to keep a dog inside that really wants to be out roaming around is really hard, and she might be grumpy, even aggressive, or anxious. Being in heat is also a messy business — like the dog having a period. Her genitals will be swollen and enlarged and there will be bleeding or discharge from the vulva: the dog will have to wear special nappy-type pants to avoid making a mess everywhere.

Another thing people don't realise is that when a female dog is in heat, the scent of her hormones will get transferred onto people living in the house, including children. Male dogs will be able to smell this and could become excited and agitated by it when you're out and about.

A female dog can have a litter of puppies and then be back into another heat cycle within six to eight weeks of giving birth. We have had dogs arrive at the sanctuary with six-month-old puppies and a set of newborns. Having puppies at a really young age can be ruinous for the mother dog's health, especially if she has a large litter.

Have I convinced you yet? Make sure your dog is desexed as soon as possible!

Dog-proofing your home

Before bringing home any new dog, but especially a puppy, you will need to pet-proof your house. Not all dogs are chewers, but most puppies are, and the last thing you want is for your precious possessions to get needle-teeth marks all over them. Taking on a dog or puppy is akin to welcoming a two-year-old child into your home. Just like toddlers, dogs have little awareness of the consequences of their actions, making pet-proofing essential for their safety and your peace of mind.

You could set aside one area of the house, such as the laundry or another tiled or lino-floored space such as a family room, where the dog will live for the first few days. You may be able to use baby gates or a playpen to cordon off an area of your living space where the dog can safely hang out. In this space make sure there is nothing poisonous that the dog can eat and nothing valuable that it can chew or damage, including any good furniture. Some dogs will express their anxiety at being in a new environment by chewing walls, doors, skirting boards, chair and table legs . . . so make sure there are as few hazards as possible, and redirect them onto chewing something more appropriate.

Make sure your garden area is also pet-proofed: that the fencing is up to scratch, and there are no chemicals, sharp objects or rubbish lying around that the dog might get into. Remove any plants that may be poisonous, too. Over its first few days at home, you will be keeping quite a close eye on your dog when it is outside anyway, but the environment needs to be as safe as possible.

If you have children, get them to pick up their toys and keep their bedroom doors closed until the dog can be trusted not to go in and help itself. Many dogs are very partial to chewing on and sucking soft toys in particular, but if they chew on or break a plastic toy, small pieces might be ingested and could cause an intestinal blockage — not to mention upsetting the child!

Keep electrical cables and phone chargers out of the dog's reach. Not only can it damage electrical cords by chewing on them, but the dog can also get a serious shock if the power is on.

You will need to supervise your new pet closely, especially at the beginning, to prevent any destructive behaviour. The dog is not being deliberately naughty — it's just exploring. But it's also up to you as the owner to set clear boundaries about what is and isn't acceptable behaviour, right from day one. It is also easier to control the environment and not let the dog have access to things it can chew — such as putting shoes away in a box with a lid, putting the TV remotes away somewhere high (not on the arm of the sofa), and closing the doors of rooms the dog is not allowed into — rather than run around behind the dog telling it off all the time, especially when it is new to your home.

Pick up the poop

Don't forget to always have poop bags on hand. They are an absolute essential: you must pick up after your dog to keep your surroundings clean and maintain a healthy environment. Responsible waste clean-up not only keeps your neighbourhood tidy but also prevents the spread of disease. Always carry poop bags during walks so you can do your part.

'Decompressing'

It usually takes about a month for a dog to 'decompress' in its new home and start to feel comfortable with its surroundings. It's very important to

create a calm and quiet environment during this time, allowing the dog to acclimatise without overwhelming it with stimulation. People who get a new dog often want to take it out straight away and show it off, or have visitors come around and see it. My advice would be to limit all interaction: don't have visitors, don't even take it out for walks for at least one week, preferably two. Just let it settle in before you start taking it out, so the dog knows where it belongs and knows where 'home' is. Some people think the dog will just go along with whatever they do, and even take it on an outing to the beach or park on the way home for the first time, but the dog can find that confusing: it needs to know where it lives and have the chance to get used to that.

When you have a new puppy, someone will need to be around most of the time for the first month or so (see below). However, even if you adopt an older dog, you will still need to take some time off work or from other commitments to spend time with it as it gets accustomed to living in your home. You can't just take it home and put it in the garden. The dog will not be familiar with its new environment and may feel frightened or lost for the first little while. Once the dog seems settled at home, gradually start to introduce outings in your immediate surroundings, so it can get used to new sights, smells and people.

Having said all this, it is also really important that after the first week or so you do start letting the dog have some time alone, so it can get used to feeling safe and secure when left at home for short periods. One of the biggest issues caused by Covid has been the separation anxiety and confusion some dogs suffered from when the lockdowns were over and their owners and other family members went back to work and school.

To make sure your dog does not develop separation anxiety, you need it to develop a healthy association with you being away from it. Start by leaving it alone in the house for just five or ten minutes while you do some gardening or walk around the block. When you come back, give it lots of love and attention, so it starts to form a positive association with you being away, then coming back. Having the dog crate-trained may also be useful (see pages 146–153); it will be happy to go into its crate and have a sleep when you're out. After a few months, you should be able to leave a puppy at home alone — in a safe space — for three or four hours; by seven or eight months this time will be a bit longer. Adult dogs may even cope with being alone for an eight-hour workday, as long as they have adequate space and stimulation, and access to an outside area, food and water.

Patience, consistency and positive reinforcement are crucial in helping your new furry family member settle in. Building a strong, loving bond with your dog from the beginning will lay the foundation for a happy, lifelong relationship.

Settling in rescue dogs

We like to keep adult dogs at the sanctuary for at least a month before we start looking for homes for them, so they have time to get used to their new surroundings. It takes a while for them to feel comfortable enough to move out of fear or protective mode and start to show their true personality and character traits. This early discomfort might cause negative behaviours like nipping, but it can also take a while for their good qualities to start to show through, once they feel less stressed and more at home. We would never take on a dog and rehome it straight away unless we already had some experience with it — the risk is too great.

The same goes for when they are adopted: it will take them some time to relax and feel comfortable in a new environment, especially if they have been rehomed several times before. Sometimes we are surprised, though: we were a bit worried about one dog that went off to its new home, thinking it might take some time to settle in and gain confidence. However, later that day the new owners sent us a picture of it happily fast asleep on the couch, as if it had lived there all its life!

Caring for puppies

Puppies can be easier to settle because their needs are simple: once they know you're the food source, they recognise that they belong to you. At the

sanctuary, all the puppies come running to the team because we are the source of food and cuddles. They know that we are where they need to go to get their needs met. Puppies will usually bond with you more quickly than adult dogs might, but initially they will miss their mothers and litter-mates, so be prepared for a few nights of crying when you first bring them home.

When you have a new puppy, someone will need to be around almost all of the time for the first month or so, and a lot of the time for the first four to six months. You shouldn't get a puppy if you're not able to be at home a lot in this early period. As well as just knowing you are nearby, the puppy will need feeding and toileting and safe socialisation, in order for it to feel safe and secure. If you absolutely have to be out for a few hours, you could arrange for someone trusted to come around and spend time with it — otherwise, plan to be spending rather a lot of time at home. A puppy should never be left on its own for more than three hours.

Once the puppy is settled at home, it is important during this early time of its development to take it out and about and introduce it to new situations. However, until the puppy is fully vaccinated (see page 194), you need to be very careful that it doesn't pick up parvo or other diseases from the soil, grass or sand, or from other dogs. When you leave your property, you will need to carry the puppy everywhere and not let its feet touch the ground. If you have to put it down so it can pee, put it on a blanket or old towel.

Similarly, it's good for the puppy to see other dogs, but don't let strange dogs sniff or lick it. You can have friends come over for a puppy play-date if their dogs are fully vaccinated, and once the puppy has had its first vaccination it's good to take it to a puppy class at the vet's or at a daycare facility, somewhere that has been cleaned properly and you know all the other puppies are vaccinated. It's important for your puppy to be socialised, but it also important to keep it safe from diseases.

Introducing children to dogs

When introducing children to a new puppy or dog, setting clear rules and boundaries is crucial for everyone's safety and well-being. Children need

to be taught how to interact with the dog gently and calmly, using a lower tone of voice to avoid overly exciting the dog. This can be really difficult for younger children, which is why adult supervision is required at all times. Running, screaming and sudden movements — like a child shrieking and putting its hands up when the dog approaches — can all trigger a dog's excitement and encourage it to chase the child, which can be dangerous. The dog will not be being deliberately naughty or aggressive — it is just picking up mixed signals and responding by instinct. Children also might not understand that most dogs don't like to be cuddled hard, held around the neck or kissed on the face.

    Teach children to respect the dog's space and understand when the dog needs some quiet time in its bed or crate, or even if it is just having a sleep in the sun. Encouraging positive interactions and rewards for calm behaviour — by the dog and the child — will foster a healthy and loving relationship that can be really special. You want your children to feel comfortable around the dog, and vice versa, but you may need to work on this to encourage them to be consistent and respectful. They should not be setting the dog up to misbehave, putting it in situations where it feels uncomfortable, or rewarding its bad behaviour.

I would never leave a young child and a dog alone in the same area, even to pop to the toilet — it takes only a split second for things to go wrong. The child might poke the dog in the eye — or, worse but sadly common, press its bum like it's a button. The dog will react in fright and the child could be scarred for life.

Remember, even the best and calmest dogs may not always understand the boundaries of play and can be caught out by the unpredictable behaviour of children, so supervising and guiding all their interactions is essential. Responsible and attentive management from the start sets the foundation for a positive and lasting bond between the entire family and their new furry friend.

Setting the hierarchy

As a pack animal, dogs are very interested in hierarchy, so it is important that right from day one they understand that the humans — including the children — are higher up the ladder than they are. This isn't being cruel or unfair to the dog: they like to know where they stand.

You don't have to assert your dominance over the dog by shouting or smacking it: it's simple things like teaching it not to jump up on the couch without being asked. The dog needs to know it is not the same as you, and it has to do what you tell it. Some dogs will try to push the boundaries, but remember: you are in charge, and you make the rules. You can't let the dog dominate you or boss you around.

Start setting rules and boundaries and demonstrating the hierarchy to puppies from day one. There's nothing wrong with putting them in their crate or in their safe room for some time out if they are being annoying or not listening.

Jessica and Kieran adopted Beauty, now named Bella, from the 'Disney' litter in May 2020. She now lives with them and their twin two-year-old sons in Henderson, Auckland.

Jessica: Growing up, I never had dogs, and was scared of them. My mum is from Fiji and there are a lot of stray dogs there, so my parents never wanted to bring a dog into their home. But through my work with the police I got used to and started to like dogs — I found they weren't so scary.

My best friend is Helen and Gavin's daughter-in-law (Sarah, see page 53), so through her I got to learn about the work they do. Watching what they posted on Facebook, I saw the ins and outs of what it takes to save so many dogs, and I became a big advocate for rescue.

Bella was part of the 'Disney' litter, and when I saw pictures of them on Facebook I fell in love with her — she was so fluffy and small. I said, 'That's our dog.' But when she first came in they thought she was a boy, and she was called Beast. We didn't want a male dog, so we went up to look at the rest of the litter.

There were eleven puppies, and we went into the garage and spent about an hour sitting with them all. I was thinking, how the heck are we supposed to choose one? But then we found out the one we liked was actually a girl, renamed Beauty, and we thought, we can't walk away from that. After all, she was the reason we were up there choosing a puppy.

We didn't have our own house — we'd just moved back to Auckland and were living with my parents at the time, so we had to win them over, too.

She is a bit of everything — bully breed crossed with Rottie. She's a medium-sized dog but weighs about 30 kg. She is all talk: she loves to bark, but if someone is actually there she freaks out. She is actually very, very gentle.

Our twin boys were born in January 2022, and bringing them home to meet her was a massive thing. We were worried about how the dog would react to not only one baby but two. But she has been amazing — she dotes on them. She understands that they are people, rather than toys, and now every morning they get up and give her a big hug in her bed. We're nearby to keep an eye on them, but she's very placid around them and plays with them and chases them around. It's amazing — she is quite a big dog, but she is such a gentle giant, she wouldn't hurt a fly.

We took her to puppy training school and she was top of her class. She's easy to train but she's smart — if you don't have a treat in your hand she knows, and she won't listen to you! Generally she's really good with loose-lead walking. She loves walking along with the pram — she's not allowed to be next to it, she has to be in front of it to protect the boys.

The biggest challenge was that it was like having a baby at first. We got her at about ten weeks old, so of course we were having to get up in the night while her bladder was growing. And entertaining her was full-on — she was very energetic as a puppy.

When we first brought her home she was highly food-oriented, having not been fed properly before she was rescued. We were fortunate to have access to one of the dog trainers at work who would do classes for police employees. We did crate-train her, but now she is allowed on the bed and she just sleeps with us.

When we first had her at home we were in lockdown and working from home quite a lot. Now she is generally by herself on a Wednesday, but either Kieran or I will work from home the rest of the time. When she was a puppy, we wouldn't leave her unattended in the house, but now we can leave her inside and literally all she does is sleep all day. She won't get up till 2 p.m.!

There are so many dogs out there that don't have homes for whatever reason. It's so important to get them desexed so they don't have puppies and end up on the side of the road in a ditch. The work Helen and Gavin do is amazing, and I have nothing but admiration for them. I see how they work with other rescues as well, and help each other out.

I just think, why would you go and spend so much money at a breeder when you can get a rescue dog that will love you just the same or even more? I love how we've had this chance to give Bella a great life. Her start in life wasn't so good, but look at her now.

Helen says:

Bella was one of a large litter of eleven unwanted pups from the Far North. The rescue that had initially taken them on was inundated with pups, so they turned to us for help.

Their mother had been scheduled for spaying when it was discovered that she was pregnant. Faced with the high cost of abortion, the decision was made to let her have the pups before proceeding with the necessary surgery.

At about six weeks old, the pups arrived at our sanctuary, having been separated from their mother. Their tiny bodies were weak and malnourished, and they were plagued by worms and fleas.

Once we had nursed them back to health, to capture the imagination of potential owners and raise funds for the sanctuary, the pups were named after Disney characters. Beauty was named after the lead female character in *Beauty and the Beast*, and was later appropriately renamed Bella.

Among the many prospective families drawn to the litter, Jessica and Kieran were captivated by Bella's sweet nature. Under their care, she flourished, her progress evident in the updates they sent, filled with tales of her training milestones and the adventures they embarked on together.

Bella's journey from an unwanted pup to a cherished member of a loving family stands as a testament to the transformative power of rescue. Her story serves as an inspiration, reminding us that every unwanted pup deserves a chance at a life filled with love and happiness.

5

Sleep

Dogs love to sleep. In fact, you may be surprised at how much time they spend snoozing. Adult dogs spend about half their lives asleep, sleeping for twelve to fourteen hours a day, while puppies need even more: in between bursts of frantic energy, they need to sleep for around eighteen to nineteen hours a day, and may only be awake for about an hour at a time, tops. Adult dogs also spend quite a lot of time every day just resting — lying around somewhere warm and comfortable, watching the world go by. It really is a dog's life!

It is important to your dog's health and well-being that it is allowed to get the sleep and rest that it needs. The old expression 'let sleeping dogs lie' isn't just about staying out of trouble; your dog needs to be left alone when it is sleeping, and kids and visitors need to understand that, too. A dog that is kept on the go all the time and denied adequate rest can become irritable and may be more likely to get sick.

If a dog is woken up suddenly from a deep sleep — by a child jumping on it, for example — it may be startled or disoriented and may react instinctively by snapping, lunging or even biting. Especially avoid having your face near the dog when it is asleep — kissing in on the head, for example — in case it gets a fright and nips you. Make sure children in particular know to avoid the dog when it is sleeping.

When a dog has had a period of exercise and/or mental stimulation, like playing fetch or tug, or some social interaction like a visitor coming by, or even just a sniff around the garden, its natural response is to drop down and take a nap. After a day running around madly at daycare, your dog may need extra sleep and rest that evening and the next day, and it's important that it gets that time. Having your dog crate-trained (see pages 146–153) can be extremely helpful when it comes to letting it get the rest and sleep it needs.

Dog beds

Most dogs are happy to sleep just about anywhere, and will just flop down on the carpet — or the couch, or your bed, if they're allowed — but it is nice for them to have a specific bed, especially if you want to restrict them to sleeping in certain areas. Older dogs especially need somewhere comfortable to rest if their joints are getting a bit worn out.

A simple, cheap dog bed will do the trick, although you can spend a lot more money on a super-soft designer bed with extra-plush fur fabric (but bear in mind your dog may simply chew it or ignore it). If it's just a simple bed, you can line it with a nice soft blanket for the dog to nest in. When choosing a dog bed, it's good to get one on the larger side, so your dog has plenty of room to move around, lie on its side and stretch out.

If your dog spends quite a lot of time outside, or enjoys lying in the sun, you might also like to get an outdoor bed for it to laze on in comfort.

Dog beds need to be washed regularly so they don't get too manky and smelly. Regularly vacuum up any hair or loose dirt, and wash the bed itself every month or so if possible. Beds with a removable, machine-washable cover are the most practical. Make sure you don't use strong cleaning products, though — you want some of the dog's natural oils to be retained in the bed so it smells right to them.

Because puppies can be energetic and prone to chewing or accidents, you can save money and stress by using second-hand bedding that's washable.

Make sure you give it a good clean before introducing it to the dog. This way, you can provide comfort without breaking the bank while your pup settles into its new home.

> ## Blanket nests
>
> You might see your dog rearranging its blanket, moving cushions and pillows around, or circling and raking at its bedding as it gets ready to go to sleep. Dogs can sometimes tear up old blankets and towels to make themselves a nice nest. This is a natural instinct, a hangover from when their ancestors pushed down grass or piled up leaves to make a bed in the wild.

Your bed?

Whether or not you choose to let your dog sleep in your bedroom, or on (or even in) your bed, is a matter of personal choice. There's something lovely and comforting about snuggling up with a warm dog, but they can also snore, fart, hog the blankets, disturb your sleep, and wake you up early in the morning. Just be aware that if you let them do it once or twice, they will consider that that is how things are going to be in the future — good luck trying to convince them to go back to sleeping elsewhere.

Normally we don't let our dogs into our bedroom overnight, but we let them in in the morning for a cuddle. Every now and then we'll leave the door open and I wake up thinking I'm paralysed, but I'm just covered in animals! If I can't get out I'll just ask Gavin for help, or he'll go make me a coffee and bring it to me so I don't have to move.

If you have small children, it's a good idea to not let the dog sleep in the bed with you, because the dog will see that as its main den and may try to guard it if the children come and get in with you. If you let it — and not the children — sleep in the bed, then it will think it has a higher place in the household hierarchy, and that it is the boss of the little people. It's fine for it to sleep on your kids' beds if that's what they and you want, but make sure you teach the dog that getting up on the bed or couch is by invitation only, not at its will. If it starts to think the bed or couch is its personal space, then it may growl at people who want to sit or lie there.

Crate training

One of the options to consider relating to your dog's sleeping and overall behaviour is whether or not to acclimatise it to a crate — which is essentially a large cage. Crate training is a preference, not an essential, but in the last ten or more years it seems to have become the done thing, and is widely talked about in dog training and ownership circles. We never used to crate-train our dogs, but once we had lots of puppies to deal with we started to crate-train them, mostly just for practical reasons. I think it can be a really effective tool if you do it correctly.

Whether or not you train your dog to spend time in a crate, and/or sleep in it, is a personal choice. There are definite advantages to it, but if your dog is completely free-range and likes to sleep with its head on your pillow (and you like that, too!), then you are not disadvantaging the dog in any way. It is probably easiest to crate-train dogs when they are puppies, while teaching them the rules of the house, but dogs can be crate-trained at any time. If you think it could be useful for your dog to sleep in a crate after it has undergone surgery, or if you are moving or travelling, you should really train it in advance — don't just put the dog in the crate on the day and expect it to cope.

You have to use it properly, too: only for the dog to sleep at night and when it needs a rest during the day. The crate can be a time-out space, but it should never be used as a punishment — it has to be a safe place for the dog, and somewhere it wants to go to. And, importantly, it has to be the dog's own personal space: once it's in there, no one else can go in, especially not kids. If you are going out for a while and don't want the dog to have the run of the house, it can be in its crate having a sleep. When the family is having dinner and you want some peace from the begging puppy eyes, the dog can have some time relaxing in its crate.

Crates are especially useful with puppies. Some people don't realise how much work puppies can be — they will just keep going and going and never want to stop playing. As I said earlier, though, they need rest, and they tend to get a bit frantic and hysterical if they don't get enough sleep, like an overtired toddler. You can put them in their crate and let them have a sleep for a couple of hours, then they will wake up refreshed and ready to go again! It's a good association for the dog to make at a young age: when I'm in here it's time to have a rest or a sleep.

If you adopt an adult dog that has not previously slept in a crate, there is no reason why it can't be trained once it is living in your house, under your rules.

A crate, not a cage

We have to be careful not to put our human interpretation onto the crate and think of it as shutting the dog in a cage — and how much we would hate that, or how cruel that seems. The dog doesn't see the crate as a jail, or as a place where it is locked up as punishment (or at least it shouldn't, so make sure it's never used for that purpose).

Dogs naturally look for enclosed spaces or hidey-holes to rest in, just as they would seek out a cave or a sheltered spot in the wild. That's why you see dogs sleeping or resting under chairs and tables — they like the sense of enclosure, and the feeling of security that provides. So by crate-training them and providing them with that safe space to rest in, you are actually doing them a favour!

You can put a blanket over the crate to make it feel more cave-like, dark and quiet. We had a very large mastiff–pit bull cross who wasn't fully crate-trained, but she loved going into her crate for a rest because it had a cover over it. She used to go in there and curl up, and seemed to love the idea of having her own space.

However, the crate should be used only for short periods of time during the day (or overnight). And once your dog is comfortable with the crate, unless you are crating it to protect it from visitors (or vice versa), the door should not be shut.

Crate advantages

There are several advantages to having your dog crate-trained. It's not just about being able to sleep in your own bed without fighting for the covers!

- If you have visitors coming over who may be less comfortable around dogs, or if your dog tends to get a bit excited when there are new people in the house, it can go and spend some time in its crate — its safe, time-out space. Once the dog is used to the crate and has come to like it, it will probably take itself in there to get away from noise or other stressful situations. It can also be put in the crate at meal-times, so it's not sitting there staring at you at the table and begging for titbits.

- Using the crate in the car can also be helpful from a safety point of view. If the dog is used to and happy to be in its crate, you can put the crate in the boot of a station wagon or SUV and it can ride safely in there.

- If your dog is staying at the vet for treatment, it is going to have to be in a crate, and the vet will love you if your dog isn't screaming and whining the whole time! If your dog needs surgery or a period of rest at home after medical treatment, it's a huge advantage if it's happy to be in a crate.

- It's also good for your dog to learn and understand that you can't be with it all the time. If your dog is used to being with you constantly and then you have to leave it for some reason, like going to hospital, knowing that it has its crate to retreat to will help it be less anxious.

Even if you don't use the crate all the time, it's a useful tool to have up your sleeve. It's a good idea to leave your dog there from time to time; that way, if it is sick or you need it to be contained, or if there are tradespeople or unfamiliar children in the house, for example, the dog knows there's a safe place to go.

Crate basics

- Make sure the crate is an appropriate size for your dog and will not be too small when it grows to its adult size, if you are starting with a puppy.

Some crates are designed to be expanded as the dog grows. The dog needs to have enough space to be able to stand, turn around easily and lie down comfortably. It doesn't need to be able to run around and play, because this is a rest space.

- When you're getting your dog used to being in the crate, have everything set up nicely, with water and maybe a treat inside and a blanket over three-quarters of it to create a snug enclosure. The goal is to make it a cosy space that the dog likes to be in. Always have a nice toy in the crate, something for it to chew on or cuddle up with.

- Encourage your dog to go inside, praise it, shut the door and walk away. If it is really stressed, start with short periods and build up to longer ones — you could go outside to do some gardening or yard work for ten or fifteen minutes — but most dogs will be fine with it. Just don't let it out while it's making a fuss, so it thinks that's the way to get let out — wait till it's quiet and calm. (That's particularly important when you're crate-training a puppy.) The key is to be consistent and persistent; you are setting some new rules and boundaries. And remember, everyone in the house has to follow the same rules: if the dog learns that one particular person will let it out if it begs, it will make that a habit. Dogs are very good at playing people off against each other!

- Leave the house for a little while and let the dog get used to it. You can leave the radio or TV on as a kind of background noise, so it is not startled by odd sounds and it feels like someone is still around (Google 'dog TV' or 'relaxing dog music' for lots of options of calming content that you can stream). When you get back, let the dog out and praise or reward it.

- When crate-training a puppy, close the door while it is still learning what the crate is for. Later, once it's grasped the idea of using the crate as a sanctuary, you can leave the door open, enabling the pup to come and go freely.

- If you are going to have the door closed, there has to be clean, fresh water in the crate, and there needs to be somewhere away from its bedding that the dog can pee if it needs to. Most dogs won't pee on their own bedding, so the dog needs to be either old enough to hold on while it's in the crate, or have a puppy pad to pee on. To start with, with their tiny little bladders, puppies can hold on for only so long, so training them to pee in one spot on a pad which can easily be removed or cleaned is ideal.

- It is OK for your dog to sleep in its crate overnight, but apart from that it should be in the crate for no more than a couple of hours at a time — when, say, you're going shopping or somewhere you can't take the dog. If you're going to be out for the whole day, it needs to have more freedom to move around. If you don't want it to have the run of the house, it should be in an outdoor area or garden, with shelter provided, or somewhere like a garage or laundry room, not in a crate. Baby gates are also useful if you want to give the dog access to some parts of the house but not others while you're out.

- For overnight stays, you need to teach the dog that the crate is its sleeping space. You may have to shut the door if it keeps coming out, until it gets the hang of it. After a while, you may find your dog puts itself to bed! Most dogs have a strong sense of routine and daily rhythm, and they know when it's bedtime. Once they've been outside for a final wee, it's into the crate and off to sleep.

Of course, the dog might use the crate during the day, and if you're happy for your dog to sleep in a bed elsewhere in the house or in with you at night, then that's fine, too. Our dogs don't sleep in crates — you'd need a pretty big crate for some of them! — but they have designated areas in the house where they sleep at night, with access to outside if they need to wee or poop.

Not all dogs like being in a crate, but most will learn to tolerate it if they know the reward at the end of it is being reunited with you. They quickly learn that when they come out of the crate they are going to get lots of love and attention. There needs to be a really positive association with the crate.

It's good for you as the owner, too — you've had some time without the dog being stuck to you like glue or hanging around under your feet, so you're more likely to give it a burst of undivided attention and affection. Once you let it out of the crate, have a play in the garden, have a tug-of-war playfight or do some training together. You can both get a lot more out of ten minutes of concentrated play after some crate time than a few hours of ignoring the dog and shooing it out of the way.

A safe space for Zeus

With our mastiff–Great Dane cross Zeus, we struggled to find a crate big enough for him. In the end, we got the biggest crate possible and took the top off it, so his head stuck out. He had to basically live in there for three months after tearing a ligament, and could only come out to go to the toilet. He wasn't happy about it, but he knew the crate was a safe place and it certainly helped his recovery in the long run. It might seem like we were being cruel to be kind, but it was better than him injuring himself further and needing another operation.

Michelle and Jim, who live close to Country Retreat, first adopted Bella (formerly Chinchilla) as a puppy, then took on ex-breeding dog Sassy as an adult. They got to know about the sanctuary and watched it grow while using the boarding kennels there for their previous dog.

We have had Bella from a puppy, from around ten weeks old. I took one look at her mother and thought, 'I want one of those puppies.' Her mum was a bearded collie and absolutely beautiful. Sassy came along in March 2023, aged three-and-a-half. She was a breeder's dog but she couldn't have puppies, so she was basically no good to them.

    We have had dogs before: our last dog was Sam, who was a fox terrier, and also a rescue. We used to live at Beachlands in Auckland, and one day I was out walking and saw a dog walking around, looking lost. He was emaciated — you could see he was skin and bones. He wasn't microchipped, so we put up signs looking for his owner, but we heard nothing, so we kept Sam for seven years before he passed away.

    We weren't going to get another dog, because losing them is so upsetting. So we weren't looking for one at the time — but they find you, you don't find them.

    I spent some time at the sanctuary helping out with the puppies — playing with them was a bit of therapy for me, really. About nine months after we lost Sam, I saw a litter I liked, and I sent some pictures to Jim, saying, 'There are some lovely puppies down here — maybe it's time to get a new dog.' One of the pictures was Chinchilla, but I was so engrossed in entertaining and cleaning up after the puppies, I didn't realise Jim had sent a reply saying, 'We'll take that one.'

We take Bella quite often to the boarding kennels, and we would always go and look at the new residents at the sanctuary. On one occasion when we took her down to the kennels for a holiday, Jim spotted a dog and fell in love. He said, 'I've been thinking about that dog, that golden retriever, the one with the big sad eyes.' Then when I went to collect Bella, he said, 'Don't forget to ask about the dog.' Helen told me Sassy's story and said, 'Do you want her?' and I said, 'I think we do.'

She was quite shy and timid and doesn't like going into new spaces, so getting her into the house was a little bit of a mission. We thought we'd give her a couple of days to see how she would settle in with Bella, but she made herself at home right away, jumping up on Bella's spot on the sofa. She's settled in quite nicely.

Bella was just a normal puppy, but it was still a big learning curve. She's not really a chewing dog, but she will come up to you with a blanket or a toy and shove it in your face as if to say, 'You need to play with me *now*.'

Before we took her on, Sassy was with Helen for quite a few months, slowly introducing her to other dogs and people. Helen did all the hard work before we got her, and now she loves humans and pats and cuddles. She still does a lot of retrieving, including things she doesn't need to retrieve. I say to her, 'I don't need those socks, but thank you.'

The two dogs are good mates and love hanging out together. They have a bit of a fight from time to time, but Sassy gives as good as she gets.

They sleep where they like — they're not crate-trained. Sometimes when I'm working from home I'll wonder where Bella is and I'll find she's gone into one of the bedrooms and is asleep on the end of the bed. She knows how to open doors — she just stands up and presses the handle. She can even open the ranch slider.

We have a nice big, fenced outdoor area and will take them down to the patch of bush nearby so they can chase possums, or we take them to the

beach at Ōmaha or Ōrewa. Sassy loves to go to the beach and meet people, while Bella likes seeing other dogs.

Once they had built the puppy pods at the sanctuary, Gavin was talking about air conditioning and Jim said, 'Why don't we see what we can do to help?' We spoke to our suppliers and asked if they were interested in donating an AC system. We got units from Temperzone and materials from Refspecs, and our company, Fonko, supplied the labour. Our guys working on the job loved it as well, playing with all the puppies. As with us, our staff are proud to have been part of a team of dedicated people ensuring the puppies and mothers have a safe and warm environment to stay in.

We chose to rescue because there are so many dogs out there that need homes. All these dogs don't ask to be born into the world, and it's a chance to give them a good life, especially when you think about the alternative and what would happen to them. I can see why Helen wants to save them all.

Whenever I hear someone is thinking about getting a dog, I always say get a rescue dog. It's not just the puppies; it's the older dogs, too, which can be harder to rehome. A lot of people are under the impression that the dog could be damaged or have problems — and they're probably right, but you can help the dog through that, and it'll reward you with love and loyalty.

Helen says:

We received a call from a rescue from the middle of the North Island: a mummy dog and twelve pups had been put into their 'drop box', where people can put their unwanted pets.

We drove for hours to get to them. The mum was exhausted, but she allowed them to feed before the long journey back home, with another stop for her to toilet and feed her pups. Once back at the sanctuary, we settled them into a nice warm room and it didn't take long for her to fall asleep.

I stayed with her the first night to help; she was so exhausted, the pups were at a higher risk of being suffocated or crushed. We do have whelping boxes, which help prevent pups getting trapped under their mother, but sometimes this isn't enough.

Fortunately, Aroha was an amazing mum, and all twelve pups survived. We don't believe all twelve pups were hers, but she took them all on and fed them all. As you can imagine, having that many pups was a handful, so we took over from Aroha when they were about five weeks old. Her poor boobies were shredded from all their sharp little teeth.

It was certainly full-on raising twelve five-week-old puppies, but they were such a lovely litter, with so many different colour variations. When Michelle spotted Bella (originally named Chinchilla), she fell in love. When she showed her husband photos of the pups, he fell for her, too. It was meant to be.

6

Feeding

One of the most important aspects of your dog's care is the food you give it. As its owner, you are responsible for not only providing it with a nutritious, balanced diet, but also for making sure it doesn't eat things it shouldn't! Many dogs are highly motivated by food and will want to eat as much as possible, whenever they can, while others are less fussed and will just eat to survive.

Food is also one of the major costs associated with dog ownership: it can cost around $1300–$1400 a year just to feed a medium-sized dog on good-quality kibble, and even more if your dog needs a special diet. Larger dogs obviously require more food: our big boy, St Bernard Jeffrey, eats 10–12 cups of biscuits *a day* as a pup (although not all at once). It is, however, important not to cut costs with dog food, as it is vital for their growth and ongoing health to get the right nutrients, not just get bulked up with fillers and carbohydrates. Giving them enough of the right kind of food will keep them satisfied and they'll be less likely to roam in search of extra calories. It's also your role as a responsible owner to make sure they don't eat too much, or have too many treats, and to maintain a healthy weight.

Feeding your dog a healthy, balanced diet will pay off in the long run with reduced vet bills and a happier dog.

Puppies

It is essential to feed puppies correctly if they are to have the best start at life. At Country Retreat, we can go through around 15 kg of puppy food a day at busy times, which really adds up! We are always grateful for donations of puppy food, to keep those hungry tummies full.

Unless your dog has had a litter which you are helping the mother take care of, by the time you take a puppy home it should already be weaned onto solid food. But if we have puppies at the sanctuary that are not being fed by their mothers (either they have been found abandoned, or she is unable or unwilling to feed them for some reason), we initially feed them specially formulated puppy milk. We use a Royal Canin puppy milk powder, which costs around $70 for 350 g, and we can go through a couple of containers a day! Newborn puppies need to be fed every two hours, because their stomach is so small they can only cope with a small amount of liquid at a time — maybe only 3–4 ml, fed to them with a bottle or syringe. Over time, we build up to feeds of around 30–40 ml, then 50–60 ml per feed by the time they are a few weeks old. I don't get much sleep when we have newborn puppies at the sanctuary: I'll often take the night shift and stay up to feed them, then try to grab some sleep during the day.

Once they are up to around 60 ml per feed (depending on the size of the puppies, that's around five or six weeks), we start encouraging them to lap the milk up, rather than feeding them from a bottle, and we start adding in some puppy mousse (super-soft food). We also soak puppy biscuits in the milk to soften them. We slowly increase the proportion of solid food and reduce the amount of puppy milk (replacing it with water) until they are around eight weeks old and are entirely on biscuits.

Very few puppies that are with their mums are fed by her for as long as eight weeks. By the time the puppies are around five weeks old, the mother dog has usually had enough of being a mobile milk bar. The puppies will be starting to get their little teeth top and bottom, so that's getting pretty uncomfortable for her! We'll see the mama dog walking around with the puppies hanging off her like little velociraptors. That's when we make sure she has some space to get away from them: we keep them in a puppy pen, and mum can jump in and feed them and then jump out again and they can't follow her. We start increasing their solid food at this time and they are usually weaned quite easily.

It's important for weaned puppies to eat specially formulated puppy kibble, because it contains more protein which supports their growth, as well as additional vitamins and minerals. It's also important not to feed them too much at once: if they eat more than their digestive systems can handle, not only will they get an upset tummy, but also a lot of the nutritional value of the food will be wasted on them, passing out in their poop. You may find that puppies eat their own poop, or that of other dogs, because there is still nutritional value in it. More frequent small feeds mean they are likely to get the most out of what they are being fed.

Eating poop

If your puppy persists in eating its own poop, put about half a teaspoon of crushed pineapple in with its dry food for a couple of days. The extra acidity will change the flavour of the poop and hopefully discourage the habit. (Only do this for a short period of time to avoid upset tummies.)

Some dogs continue to eat poop into adulthood, but this is a bad trait as they could pick up all kinds of diseases. Don't let them snack on poop when out for a walk — keep a close eye on them when they are exploring, and discourage them with a firm 'leave it' command.

If your dog starts eating poop when it didn't before, then it's worth checking in with your vet: it may not be getting the nutrition it needs from its food due to gastrointestinal issues, parasites, or other medical problems including diabetes or dementia.

Puppies can be transitioned onto an adult dog food at around a year or eighteen months old, depending on the size of the dog — bigger dogs take longer to get to their adult size. I encourage owners to keep their young dogs on puppy food for at least eighteen months so they can get the most out of that extra goodness. If they go on eating it as adult dogs, however, they may start to put on extra weight.

If cost is an issue, just try to keep them on a high-quality puppy food for as long as you can; then, when they are ready to transition, they may be able to do well on a less-expensive adult brand. That little bit extra you spend on quality food when they are growing and developing may end up saving you money on vet bills further down the track.

Adult dogs

We feed all our adult dogs twice a day — the dogs in the sanctuary and the ones staying at the kennels, even if they are fed once a day at home. This means they get the nutrition they need without eating too much at one time, and their gut has time to process it properly. Some people feed their adult dogs only once a day and that's also fine, especially if the dog is quite small. If you have a large dog like our boy Jeffrey, it wouldn't be safe for him to eat all his food in one meal; it can lead to digestion problems, and in rare cases to a dangerous complication known as bloat (see page 214).

For all our dogs, we use the best-quality kibble we can get: brands like Hill's Science Diet, Black Hawk and Royal Canin. We don't tend to feed our dogs soft food or dog roll. If you do want to feed your dog canned food or dog roll, you need to get a good-quality one that looks and feels like actual meat. The cheaper ones contain a lot of water and fillers, and can be nutritionally poor.

Sometimes we add a bit of dog roll to kibble if we have an older dog or one we need to fatten up a bit, especially if they need something softer to eat. We pop a little bit of dog roll on top as a treat to encourage them to eat.

If you are feeding kibble alone, with no wet-food component, the dog needs to have access to plenty of water at all times. Again, it's not good for it to drink too much water at once, so little and often is the key. Make sure you clean its water bowl and top it up with fresh water regularly.

If you have multiple dogs, you will need to work out how to feed them all fairly without them potentially stealing each other's food, and some dogs

overeating while other dogs miss out. You may have to feed them one at a time, while the other dog waits in its crate or in another room.

While some dogs will eat whatever is put in front of them until the bowl is empty or is taken away, some dogs are more grazers. I am not keen on letting dogs snack and graze, however; I put the food out, and if they haven't eaten it after fifteen minutes or so, I take it back up. It stops our other dogs from eating it, plus it stops flies from getting on it as it sits around. They will soon learn when breakfast and dinner time is, and that they need to eat when the food is available.

Some dogs are also fussy about what they will and won't eat, and may have a strong preference for a certain brand or flavour of food. You need to be careful, too, when transitioning between foods, especially with young dogs, so their stomachs can get used to the new food. When moving from puppy food to adult dog kibble, for example, start by mixing the two foods together, increasing the proportion of adult food over a period of days so they have time to adjust. We usually start with a 70:30 ratio of old food to new, then 50:50, and 30:70, making sure there are no tummy upsets before we move 100 per cent to the new food.

Feeding rescue dogs

We get some rescue dogs that have been starved or underfed all their lives, and they will just eat and eat until they vomit. We also have to be careful when introducing them to proper food because it can be too rich for their tummies and come out the other end as diarrhoea! In these cases, we feed the dog smaller amounts every couple of hours and build up the amount it can cope with, rather than give it big meals.

Raw feeding

I am personally not keen on raw food for dogs, and certainly not for puppies, but it is a matter of personal preference. I would encourage you to do some thorough research on the topic — it's not just a matter of feeding them raw meat. Dogs have a wide range of nutritional needs that need to be met for them to stay healthy — they are no longer wolves running around in the wild, killing other animals to eat! Well-designed raw diets include other foods such as yoghurt, eggs, bones, and organ meats like tripe. You can get pre-packaged raw-food mixes, and some companies will put together packages of everything you need, but it does take a lot more time and energy.

If you are going to feed your dog some raw foods as well as kibble, don't put the food in the same bowl or feed them both at the same meal, as you will be mixing acid and alkali foods and can give your dog a stomach upset.

One advantage of raw feeding is that it removes all fillers and grains from the dog's diet, and may be a good option if your dog has intolerances to these foods. It also reduces the amount of poop that's produced. But as we said, do your research first and be prepared to have to put in quite a lot of time, money and effort to do it properly.

Maintaining a healthy weight

It's really important for your dog's overall health, and especially the state of its bones, muscles and joints, that it maintains a healthy weight. A lot of dogs out there are overweight: we are now in the habit of seeing bigger, chubbier dogs out and about, and a healthy-weight dog can actually look quite skinny in some people's eyes. Talk to your vet if you're not sure what your dog's ideal weight should be — it may be lower than you think.

You can also make your own assessment of your dog's body condition by making three basic checks:

- Run your hands over the area of its ribcage and note what you can feel.

- Look at your dog side-on, getting down to its level to have a good look at its profile.

How much food?

Some dogs are always keen for food. They don't seem to have natural hunger and fullness cues — given half a chance, they will always eat too much, and act like they're absolutely starving each time they get fed. Don't get sucked into thinking your dog needs more food just because it's giving you those puppy eyes. Speaking of puppies, it's quite easy to over-feed them, which is just a waste of food — again, you may need to feed them little and often to make sure they are getting the best out of their food and don't just vacuum up whatever is put in front of them.

How much food a dog needs each day relates to its size, age and activity level. Here is a rough rule of thumb for how much dry food to give a dog getting an average amount of exercise each day. (Note: this is a total daily amount; if you're feeding twice a day, split the total into two):

Dog weight	Cups
under 5 kg	1/3–1
5–10 kg	1–1 1/3
10–15 kg	1 1/3–2
15–22 kg	2–2 2/3
22–35 kg	2 2/3–3 1/3
35–45 kg	3 1/3–4 1/4
45 kg plus	4 1/4, plus 1/4 cup for each 4.5 kg of body weight

Another good rule of thumb is that the size of a dog's stomach is roughly the same size as the top of its head, between the ears. It's a lot smaller than you might think! Added to that, kibble swells considerably when wet — so what may look like a paltry amount in the bowl will grow to a much larger volume in the stomach. Like humans, dogs' stomachs can stretch over time to accommodate more food if they are overfed, so it's good to think about how much they actually need, and feed them a healthy, appropriate amount.

🐾 Look down at your dog from above.

On a dog with a healthy body condition:

🐾 The ribs can be easily felt, with a minimal layer of overlying fat. If you have a short-haired dog you should be able to just see the ribcage.

🐾 It will have a noticeable tummy tuck when looked at from side on — its undercarriage shouldn't be a straight line from chest to belly.

🐾 A clear waistline can easily be seen from above — the dog should have an hourglass shape, with the shoulders and rear end being wider than its waist.

If your dog is either under- or overweight, talk to your vet about how you can best adjust its diet and improve its condition.

Remember to keep dog 'treats' to a minimum, as the calories can start to add up if you are rewarding your dog frequently with food. Again, dogs are not human — they don't need a little something extra for dessert. By all means use treats to enhance training, but keep an eye on how much extra food your dog is eating on top of its regular diet.

Foods to avoid

Given the opportunity, dogs will eat all sorts of foods, some of which at the very least are not good for them, and at worst can make them ill or even kill them.

Human food in general is a no-no, as it is often way too salty, sugary or fatty for dogs to digest. It's also likely to be high in calories; regularly feeding your dog scraps from the table or just a little bit of what you're eating can easily make your dog put on weight. The best rule is to not give it any food other than dog food, and to feed it only at its meal-times.

Dogs are omnivores rather than pure carnivores, and can enjoy fresh fruit and vegetables as part of their meals, but there are some seemingly 'healthy'

foods which should also be avoided. Carrots and apple can be fed in small quantities, and can help to keep your dog's teeth clean and improve its breath. Just make sure you remove the apple core and all the seeds. A bit of grated carrot is a good way to add fibre to the dog's diet if its poop is a bit soft. Many dogs also like the odd strawberry or blueberry, and a bit of orange, tomato, mango, pineapple or watermelon — but a little bit is enough (and take the seeds out of the watermelon). Peas, beans, and cooked kūmara and potato can be eaten by most dogs. A little peanut butter is also a good treat, but pick one that is as natural as possible and make sure it doesn't include the sweetener Xylitol (which is toxic to dogs) or too much salt or sugar.

Yummy peanut butter canine cookies

You can make your own dog treats using simple household ingredients. This recipe comes from Raewynne, owner of rescue dog Pippa (see pages 178–187) and one of our volunteers.

1 cup flour
½ cup rolled oats
½ cup cooked, mashed kūmara
1 egg
4 tablespoons peanut butter

Heat oven to 180°C.

Place flour and oats in a bowl and stir together. Slowly mix in the kūmara mash, egg and peanut butter.

Knead dough, adding water if needed, until texture is firm. Roll dough until 0.5 cm thick. Cut into squares (or shapes, such as bones).

Place dough pieces on lightly greased baking paper. Cook for 20 minutes or until golden and firm.

No to these!

Some foods should *never* be fed to dogs, including:

- 🐾 **Chocolate:** This is a biggie. A reasonable amount of dark chocolate can kill a small dog, but no amount of any type of chocolate is good for a dog. If your dog gets into your chocolate stash, get in touch with the vet as soon as possible so it can be induced to vomit up what it's eaten as soon as possible.

- 🐾 **Grapes and raisins:** These can cause a toxic reaction and kidney damage in many dogs. Better to be safe than sorry: if your dog eats grapes or raisins by accident, call your vet urgently.

- 🐾 **Onions and garlic:** Another reason not to feed your dog off your plate, as many human foods contain these substances.

- 🐾 **Mushrooms:** Even varieties we consider edible may be dangerous to your dog.

- 🐾 **Milk and dairy products:** Dogs are lactose-intolerant, but they may be able to tolerate (and love) small amounts of cheese and unsweetened Greek yoghurt.

- 🐾 **Nuts:** Whole nuts may choke a dog and can cause intestinal blockages. Also, the high oil and fat content of nuts can cause vomiting and diarrhoea. Macadamia nuts are poisonous to dogs.

- 🐾 **Cooked bones:** Only ever feed your dog raw bones, as cooked bones are brittle and can splinter. But also be careful with feeding your dog raw meat, especially chicken, and raw eggs, as these can contain dangerous bacteria such as *Salmonella* and *E. coli*.

- 🐾 **Chewing gum:** Obviously you wouldn't feed this to your dog, but make sure it doesn't steal it from your bag. The sweetener Xylitol used in many sugar-free gums is poisonous to dogs, and if they swallow gum it can get stuck in their digestive system.

- 🐾 **Avocado:** The skin and pit contain persin, a naturally occurring fungicide that can poison your dog. The pit is also a choking hazard.

Raewynne and Pippa

Raewynne is a regular volunteer at Country Retreat, helping out five mornings a week. She adopted American Staffordshire bull terrier–Labrador cross Pippa (originally Sundae from the 'Dessert' litter) in 2021.

I've been volunteering here for about three-and-a-half years. Our previous dog had died and I had all her stuff, and I was looking for somewhere to donate it to. The vet suggested Country Retreat, so I came here and met Helen and Gavin. At that stage they only had the garage in use as a rescue centre, and a litter of puppies had just come in. I said I'd quite like to volunteer and Helen said, 'Why don't you come tomorrow?' I asked what time and she said 'Seven a.m.' I was like, 'OK, right!' I've been on the morning shift ever since.

We had been without our previous dog, Astro, for about eighteen months, and I had been volunteering here for about a year. My husband was due to retire, so we thought we'd wait till he had retired until we got another dog. Pippa was one of a litter that I got to know, and she seemed a lot quieter than the rest — although it didn't turn out that way!

I've always had rescue dogs — I was a volunteer at the SPCA for eighteen years, and we got our previous dog from there. Seeing all the litters of puppies that come in here, we were never going to look anywhere else.

There have been times when I've thought I shouldn't have got another dog so soon. She's so different to our old dog in temperament, so it has been a challenge. We've trained her like our other dogs and she's very obedient, but she does think she has rights! You can tell her a thousand times to get out of the kitchen and she'll go, but she'll just come back again. She absolutely has a mind of her own.

She also has hip dysplasia, but we can't do anything about it. If she had surgery, she would probably still get arthritis later in life. She can run and play but we have to limit that, and if she overdoes it she will be sore later on. She will just need a bit more help later in life.

She's turned out to be a really great dog. She has a couple of funny traits — if she's off-lead and someone halfway down the beach is throwing a ball, she's gone! But she's great around the house, and never chews anything apart from her own toys.

I love that Pippa is determined. She's always really, really happy. She's great with our cat, great with other people. We can leave the garage door open and it's not far from the road, but she'll just sit there and watch people go by.

Rescues like Country Retreat fill a huge gap. Just imagine if there were no rescues — all those puppies would be dead, and pregnant mums would be wandering on the street. Not a lot of rescues will take two- or three-day-old puppies, because for a couple of weeks they need care around the clock, so what Helen and Gavin do is really important.

Unfortunately, there is so much need for rescue. It was good to see on TV recently that the SPCA was going up north with their desexing bus — they should be up there 24/7. I have a sister who runs two charity shops in Putāruru called PAWS, through which she raises money solely to pay for animals to be desexed and to run desexing clinics. She's been doing it for twelve years.

The hardest thing I find is that the people who dump these dogs and puppies do it in such a way that they're not caught. They never get prosecuted, there's no comeback. I often think that people who are cruel to animals should be made to work in a rescue shelter, so they might get to understand that it's not OK, and that animals are not something that you can mistreat — they're something you can come to love.

Helen says:

Pippa's mum, Bonnie, was transferred from another rescue and arrived at the sanctuary heavily pregnant. They had found Bonnie roaming the streets and had done an amazing job caring for her, but they lacked the facilities and resources to see her pregnancy through. Bonnie was an immediate hit with our volunteers — sweet, affectionate and gentle despite her rough exterior.

The day Pippa was born was a heartstopper. Bonnie struggled through her labour. She was trying to push the pups out, but nothing was happening. We timed her contractions and, after regular contact with our local vets, we made the decision that she needed to be taken in to ensure her puppies were not in distress.

Upon examination, the vets said it looked as though a puppy — unlikely to still be alive — was wedged in the birth canal, and was now compromising the life of both its siblings and its mother. The best course of action was going to be a C-section delivery. The team of nurses and sanctuary helpers scrubbed up to assist with the incoming pups.

The pups started to emerge, nurses and helpers frantically rubbing them with towels in place of their mum (still in surgery), willing them to start breathing. One by one their little cries brought relief to everyone in the room.

Finally, the pup wedged in the birth canal was removed — a little girl. She weighed 530 g, and there was no chance that she could have been born naturally. Against all odds, the little wedge was alive, and after a vigorous rub she spluttered into life. All eight puppies were taken to their mum for milk as she came round from surgery.

Little Wedge, as she was affectionately known, was named Sundae, as part of our 'Dessert' litter. She would become Pippa, and has grown to be an amazing dog. We love it when Pippa stops by for a cuddle — the little wedge, our little miracle.

7

Keeping your dog healthy

Like any animal, a dog is susceptible to a range of injuries, illnesses and ailments. Good animal husbandry — giving it good food, making sure it gets enough exercise and mental stimulation, and keeping it in a safe environment at home and when out and about — can prevent some of them. But dogs will be dogs! They will eat things they shouldn't, they will catch bugs off other dogs, and they can injure themselves when playing. It's a lot like having a child! So you need to keep a close eye on your dog, and respond to any changes in behaviour that you see.

Dogs can be good at hiding when they are feeling unwell or are in pain, so pay attention to changes in eating patterns and energy levels. They won't necessarily communicate with you that something is wrong, coming to you and whimpering like they do in the movies, but their behaviour will give you clues. Key things to look out for are if the dog is sleeping more than usual, being less social and wanting to hide or stay away from you, or if it is off its food.

You will know your dog best, and will probably get a 'gut feeling' when something is wrong with your canine companion. A quick call or trip to the vet to check things out and get either reassurance or treatment could be worth its weight in gold further down the track, instead of waiting and running the risk of the dog getting sicker.

Just a note here: obviously I am not a veterinarian, and the following information is no substitute for talking to a professional if you have any concerns at all about your dog's health.

Know your dog

Any change in a dog's behaviour is significant, because most dogs don't like to show they are ill. That said, some dogs are complete drama queens! We had one dog staying at our kennels that wouldn't stop screaming, so we took him off to the vet for tests and x-rays. They showed nothing major was wrong, so we gave him some pain relief, but he just wouldn't stop carrying on. The next day, the owner came to pick him up and said he'd probably just stepped on a stone and bruised his foot — he was a complete wuss like that! My advice is, if you know your dog is a bit like this, when you leave it with someone else, let them know what to expect.

By and large, if your dog is either crying or a lot more vocal than usual, or, on the opposite end of the scale, a bit quiet or lethargic, and there is no other reason for it (you haven't been for a big run, for example), your dog is probably showing you that there is something wrong, either deliberately or subconsciously.

If you see your dog doing something odd on and off — for example, limping intermittently, breathing in a funny pattern, or chewing its wrist — try to make a video of the behaviour, in case it acts normal when it gets to the vet. Dogs don't want to be seen as the weak link in the pack and will usually try to hide any problem when in an unfamiliar situation.

Pet insurance

As well as giving your dog a healthy diet (see chapter 6) and the right amount of exercise and rest (see chapter 5), you need to take it in for regular vet checks and vaccinations, and have a schedule for parasite treatment (fleas, worms and ticks — see page 195). Prevention is better than cure, and if your dog does get sick or injured, veterinary care is expensive. You don't want to be faced with the choice of having to find a large amount of money or allowing your dog to suffer or even be put to sleep because you can't afford the treatment. Some quite common operations can cost literally thousands of dollars, and vets deserve to be paid promptly for their work.

I encourage anyone who can afford it to invest in pet health insurance. If you don't feel you can afford the monthly premiums, or you'd rather save independently, put some money aside regularly in a special account for doggy medical problems.

Most pet insurance policies don't cover vaccinations or standard vet check-ups — and, in fact, these checks and vaccinations may have to be done for the insurance policy to be valid. You will be able to choose the excess you pay on the policy, which will affect the premium you pay — for example, you might agree to pay the first $200 of any treatment, but be covered for the rest, which could be thousands more. You can also choose to be covered solely for serious conditions or surgery, which will reduce premiums but leave you with the majority of minor vet bills.

The premium will also vary according to the dog breed, as some types of dog are more susceptible to certain illnesses and injuries than others — for example, heart conditions for boxers, or skin and eye problems with shar peis. You may run into issues with mixed-breed dogs, too — some people believe mixed breeds are more hardy, but having genes from different breeds can mean potentially bad genes can be inherited, too. This can be quite hard for rescues, because about 98 per cent are mixed breeds. For example, a dog might have some shar pei in it, but also terrier or bulldog or other breeds with their own problems, and you may be excluded for a range of different conditions. A good insurance agent will be able to talk through a suitable level of cover for your dog. Ideally, you want insurance that will cover your dog completely.

Another tip is to get insurance as soon as you get the dog or puppy — don't wait until something major has happened. Not only will you not be covered for the initial incident, but you may also find that condition will be excluded in the future. If your dog is insured from puppyhood, you are less likely to run into such problems. Some insurance policies will cover dogs only up to a certain age, or exclude certain breeds of dogs once they get older and are more likely to develop health issues.

So, look for policies that cover whole of life, and don't ramp up hugely in cost as the dog gets older. Yes, older dogs are more likely to suffer from conditions like arthritis and cancers, but it should be averaged out over the dog's lifetime.

Do your research, talk to other dog owners about their experiences with various companies, and always read the fine print to find out what is covered and what is excluded. You may not like to think about your dog needing extensive and expensive vet care, but it's better to be safe than sorry.

Breed-specific health issues

Some ailments are breed-specific, and some breeds are more likely to develop certain health issues than others. For example, breeds such as bulldogs and pugs that are 'brachycephalic' (with a shortened, flattened head and snout) are more likely to have respiratory problems, due to the bone structure of the skull, which makes it hard for them to breathe properly. German shepherds and other large dogs are more likely to suffer from hip dysplasia and arthritis. Cocker spaniels and other breeds with floppy, furry ears are susceptible to ear infections.

It's worth doing your research into breed-specific issues when choosing what type of dog to get, so you can be informed and keep an eye on symptoms developing in your pet.

Vaccinations

Vaccinations are not mandatory, but they are the right thing to do if you want to look after your dog's health. Diseases like parvovirus (see page 201) are usually fatal for puppies, and there is so much of it around in the environment, your dog can easily catch it. Likewise, canine cough (also known as kennel cough) is highly infectious, and while it may not make your dog horribly unwell, it is nonetheless very unpleasant, and it would be irresponsible of you as a dog owner to allow the disease to spread.

Like human vaccinations, the inoculations work by 'priming' your puppy's immune system against certain viruses and bacteria, so it is better prepared to fight the illness if it encounters it later. Puppies get some antibodies through their mother's milk, but once they are weaned they need to start developing their own internal protection through vaccination.

In New Zealand there is a core vaccination that covers against canine distemper, parvovirus (parvo), infectious hepatitis and canine parainfluenza. Most dogs are also vaccinated against canine leptospirosis (lepto), and infectious tracheobronchitis (canine cough). Your dog will have to be vaccinated against these last two as well as the core diseases if they are going to be with other dogs in a daycare or kennels, and just for their overall well-being. (See pages 200–203 for more on these illnesses.)

Vets' vaccination schedules vary, but usually your pup will need three sets of initial vaccinations, four or so weeks apart, followed up by an annual booster. It is important to remember that your dog's protection is not complete until *eleven days following the last core vaccination*. Up to this time, your pup should be kept at home or carried when out and about, avoiding any direct contact with unvaccinated dogs.

Keep a clear record that you can share with anyone who is going to be caring for your dog — your vet should give you a little booklet and stick the vaccination vial stickers in there for you, with the date they were administered.

There is a cost associated with vaccinations — around $300 for the initial course for puppies, and around $150 a year after that — and this is not usually covered by pet insurance. However, a single trip to the vet if your dog contracts one of these diseases will cost you at least $100, so it makes sense to invest in your dog's health and be proactive.

Your dog may be more sleepy or less active than normal following a vaccination; this is normal, and the dog should come right within twenty-four hours.

Parasites

All dogs need treatment for fleas, worms, ticks and mites on a regular basis. All these parasites can have a negative effect on your dog's health, and there's also the risk of passing these pests on to other pets and human family members, especially children.

Talk to your vet about the best treatment for your dog, whether it is a separate medication that tackles each parasite or a single all-round treatment. We recommend buying treatments from a specialist pet shop or your vet, rather than the supermarket, to make sure you are getting good-quality, effective products. They will be slightly more expensive, but it's worth it to keep your dog free from problem parasites. We've had puppies come to the sanctuary that had been treated with a supermarket product, yet were so sick they nearly died. Your vet can recommend worm and flea treatments that will offer a full spectrum of coverage and be right for your particular dog or puppy.

Carefully read the paperwork that comes with the treatment, as the size of the dose will relate to the weight of the dog, and some can't be given to small dogs or puppies. Some breeds may also have negative reactions to some products: for example, English collies ('Lassie' dogs) can't be given certain flea treatments, as many of them have a specific gene mutation that makes the active ingredient poisonous to them. Again, talk with your vet if you have any concerns.

A monthly dose of a combined flea, tick and worm product should cost around $25–$35, depending on the size of your dog.

Fleas

Dogs and fleas are a match made in heaven. These little insects, only 1–2 mm long, live for only a week or two but can be very annoying, living in your dog's fur and biting through its skin to drink its blood. Females can lay up to 40 eggs a day, which hatch into tiny larvae and live in the environment — in dog bedding, or in your couch or carpet — before emerging as adult fleas and starting the cycle again. They love warmth and humidity, so summer is peak flea season, when the larvae mature and make the most of their brief time as adults.

There are a lot of larvae in the environment and it's easy for your dog to pick up fleas.

Fleas can transmit diseases, but are also a major irritant. You may not be able to see the fleas, but your dog may be scratching itself or grooming more than usual, and may also get red patches or scabs on its skin.

The best way to prevent an infestation is to regularly use an anti-flea treatment; consistent use is important, as it helps break the flea's reproductive cycle. If your dog has fleas, you will need to treat your home as well as the dog, to get rid of adult fleas and eggs. Make sure that the flea treatment you choose also covers mites (see below).

Mites

These tiny pests are arachnids, distantly related to spiders. Around 1 mm long, they burrow into a dog's skin and can cause irritation and hair loss. Mite infestations can lead to a condition called mange, where the dog develops bald patches, dandruff-like flaking, sore and red areas of skin, and sometimes crusting. To diagnose what's going on, your vet will take a scraping of the skin area and look for mites under a microscope. Again, the best form of treatment is prevention: give your dog regular anti-mite treatment to keep the pests away.

Some mites live inside the dog's ear canal. They require a live animal host to survive, and they are passed very easily from animal to animal. If your dog has ear mites, you might see it shaking its head and scratching its ears more than usual, as their presence is very irritating and can cause a lot of discomfort.

If your dog gets ear mites, you will have to treat your home environment to make sure you kill the mites there, too, but unfortunately they are easy to pick up in the outdoor environment.

Worms

It is important to treat your dog regularly for worms, to stop you and your family becoming infested. Worms are passed from dog to dog, or dog to human, by ingestion of the eggs, which means they are easily passed on to children, who tend to put their hands in their mouth. It's one of the reasons I'm not keen on seeing dogs anywhere near children's playgrounds — not just because some kids might be scared of dogs, but also because they can accidentally pass worms on to the kids. It's also another good reason to pick up your dog's poop, and to prevent your dog from eating other dogs' leavings.

If your dog has worms, it may have no symptoms, but you might see them in its poop, like little white bits of rice or long strands like spaghetti. In bad cases, the dog might be lethargic, have diarrhoea or vomiting, and lose weight despite eating. Go and see your vet and get it checked out. The vet may want you to bring along a stool (poop) sample.

In New Zealand the most common types of worms are roundworms, hookworms, whipworms and tapeworms. Roundworms are the most common type in domestic dogs. They live in the dog's intestines, and while most dogs won't show any sign of being infected, they will be able to pass the worms on to other dogs and humans through worm eggs in their poop. In severe cases, however, especially in puppies, these worms can travel from the gut to the heart, lungs and brain. It's heartbreaking to see the state of some puppies that come in to our rescue, which can be blind or have difficulty walking because they are so infested with worms, and can actually die from it. Puppies can pick up roundworms through their mother's milk if she is not treated, so it is a priority for us to treat new puppy arrivals for worms as soon as possible.

Whipworms, hookworms and tapeworms are less common in New Zealand but no less troublesome. Again, prevention is better than cure, so deworm your dog every three months with a good-quality, all-round worming product.

Ticks

It's quite common for dogs to pick up blood-sucking ticks, especially if you live in a rural area where there are farm animals around. Ticks, like mites, are arachnids. They are horrible things, and sometimes we can spend hours pulling them off dogs. We had one rescue dog that came in with her head covered in ticks, around her eyes and in her ears. She was also very anaemic because of all the ticks drinking her blood. I've never seen anything like it — fortunately.

Ticks start off tiny, but they can swell up to the size of a pea once they've been sucking your dog's blood for a while. They might look like a dot or a wart on your dog's skin, but if you look closely, you might see their little legs. They are usually nestled in around your dog's head and neck, or near the feet. They can't jump or fly — they just drop onto your dog from foliage or are picked up from long grass.

When dealing with a tick, take great care to remove it entirely, so that its mouthparts don't remain embedded in the dog's skin. Ticks should fall off if the dog is given an oral anti-tick treatment, or you can get a special tick-removal tool from your vet. You can also suffocate a tick by putting Vaseline on a cotton bud and rubbing it on the pest.

Some flea treatments also guard against ticks, so look for a good all-round product.

Parasite control: the basics

Depending on what type of product you use, here is a general guide:

- Puppies need to be wormed every two weeks from 2–12 weeks old. They then need to be wormed every month until they are six months of age.

- Adult dogs need to be wormed every three months — or monthly in the case of some combo treatments that cover fleas as well as worms.

- 🐾 Never give your dog a topical treatment (to be dabbed on the skin) to swallow, as this can be fatal.

- 🐾 Fleas, mites and ticks tend to require a monthly treatment.

- 🐾 Make sure you give your dog the correct dose for its weight.

- 🐾 Set up a reminder in your phone, or use an app, to notify you when treatment is due.

Common illnesses

Some diseases, such as parvovirus and canine cough, can affect any dog. While for many healthy dogs, especially if they have been vaccinated, getting an infection is an unpleasant inconvenience which they can get over with veterinary treatment, diseases such as parvo can be fatal for puppies or older dogs, which have weaker immunity.

Dogs that spend time in social situations, such as doggy daycare or overnight stays at kennels, are more likely to contract infectious diseases from their canine companions, but even dogs that spend most of their time at home can pick up diseases when out on walks in their local environment. For example, canine cough is so infectious that dogs only need to touch noses or drink from a shared water bowl to spread it.

Canine cough

Unfortunately, even if dogs are vaccinated they can still catch a mild case of canine cough, and it is still very common. It is also highly infectious. The old name 'kennel cough' made people think dogs caught it only if they were in kennels, when in fact they can easily get it from another dog at any time, or from picking up a stick that another dog has had in its mouth — that's how contagious it is.

Because there are various strains and combinations of viruses that can cause it, even if your dog is immunised it might still get canine cough. It might be sick for five or so days, with a runny nose and coughing, but not be too unwell overall. If your dog is unvaccinated, however, an infection may cause serious respiratory problems.

The most common symptom is a dry, harsh cough, which can last for a few weeks, along with retching and gagging up frothy white saliva. Treatment is like for a common human cold — rest, fluids and taking it easy. Be sure to keep your dog away from all other dogs while it is still coughing. Your vet may prescribe an antibiotic if they think there is a bacterial infection, but it is usually mostly viral. Call ahead and tell them if your dog has canine cough symptoms, as they will want to examine the dog in isolation rather than risk bringing it into the clinic.

Leptospirosis

Leptospirosis, or lepto, is a bacterial disease that can also be passed to humans, and can cause serious health problems such as kidney damage, meningitis, liver failure, and even death. The bacterium spreads through rat and cow urine and can contaminate soil, water or food through contact. People and pets who live on farms are more likely to be exposed to it, but even if you don't live in the countryside you can still catch it. Dogs in the South Island aren't usually vaccinated against lepto because it is not considered a risk there.

Symptoms include fever, vomiting and diarrhoea, loss of appetite, weakness and joint stiffness. Lepto can be treated with antibiotics if it is caught early enough but the illness usually requires intensive care in hospital. If your dog contracts it, you will need to keep the house scrupulously clean to ensure no humans catch it.

Parvovirus

Parvo is a virus that attacks the dog's digestive system and sometimes the heart. It's spread through the vomit and poop of infected dogs. It is unfortunately very common in New Zealand currently, due to lower vaccination rates during Covid, and outbreaks tend to occur in summer, as the virus is more likely to survive in warmer weather. It can persist in the environment literally for years — in the soil, on grass and on sand on the beach. We won't let a dog go to a home where there has been parvo in the past five years.

It's a horrible disease, and a horrendous way for a pup to die. It causes chronic diarrhoea and vomiting, leading to lethargy and dehydration, and eventually the whole body just gives up. Little puppies don't usually survive. It can be treated, but it's both expensive and awful for the dog, which will usually have to stay at the vet for intravenous fluids and medication.

If your puppy is out of sorts and is vomiting or has diarrhoea contact your vet as soon as possible. It may simply have eaten something that it shouldn't have, but it's better to be safe than sorry.

Sometimes rescue dogs and puppies that haven't been vaccinated can be brought in already with parvo, which is a massive problem — the pound or shelter has to be closed and the dogs that have it are put down, which I find heartbreaking to think about. All new dogs and puppies that come to our sanctuary are isolated and tested for parvo. It is another expense for us, but it's better than the risk of spreading the disease.

Distemper and canine hepatitis

Fortunately, thanks to vaccination, both distemper and canine hepatitis are now uncommon in New Zealand. Distemper causes a watery discharge from the eyes, followed by fever, coughing, lethargy and vomiting, followed by nervous-system damage which can cause convulsions and seizures. Canine hepatitis is caused by a virus and causes liver disease, which leads to neurological symptoms and often death. Your dog is unlikely to catch either of these diseases, but talk to your vet if you are at all concerned.

Cancer

Dogs can get almost all types of cancer, and unfortunately it's one of the biggest killers of our canine companions. As with humans, dogs are now living longer because of better nutrition and care, so they are more likely to get cancers associated with advanced age. Fortunately, better medical care and more advanced treatments now give them a better chance of surviving, but even if a dog undergoes successful treatment, there is no way of knowing how much longer it will live afterwards, or if the cancer will come back.

Among the most common types affecting dogs are skin cancers, such as melanomas, mast cell tumours and squamous cell carcinomas. These can affect all breeds, but mast cell cancers are more common in breeds such as boxers, Boston terriers and retrievers, and squamous cell carcinomas are found more often in pale-coloured, short-haired dogs such as bull terriers and Dalmatians. Unlike in humans, canine melanoma is usually found on dark-skinned dogs, but the tumours can be benign.

Lymphomas (blood cancers) are also quite common in dogs. They can be hard to pick up and are often not diagnosed until it is too late to save the dog. We had a dog at the kennels who we noticed doing black poop, like tar. We took him to the vet straight away, because that is a sign of intestinal bleeding. When the vet opened him up to see what was going on, they came back to say, 'We don't think we should revive him,' because they had found so much cancer inside him. Yet the day before he had been running around and playing happily — he just gave no signs that he was unwell.

Check your dog regularly for lumps and keep an eye on any sores that don't heal, unusual swelling, unexplained weight loss, or difficulty eating or swallowing, all of which may be related to swollen lymph glands.

If your dog is found to have cancer, even if treatment is possible, it will be expensive. Eventually, you also may have to make the difficult call of when enough is enough and it is time to let your dog go and have it euthanised. No one wants to see their dog in pain and suffering, and there will come a point when it is kinder to allow it to die. With our dog Zeus, we spent $10,000 on his care and he still passed away. Many people would not have that kind of money to spend on their dog's medical bills, which is another good reason to get pet insurance.

> ### Helping it down
>
> Fortunately, dogs are much easier to give medication to than cats. A lot of dogs will take any pill, even quite large ones, if it's disguised in a chunk of cheese or another treat food!

Common ailments

Skin issues

Dogs need regular grooming to keep not only their coat but also their skin healthy. This will range from the odd bath and a brush for a short-coated dog to professional clipping and stripping for dogs with long hair or double coats.

Research the best type of brush for your dog's coat, and when you give it a bath, use a gentle, dog-specific shampoo that also suits your dog's coat type. Avoid using human shampoos, as they can be harsh on your pet's skin. Some dog types need to be washed more than others: oily-coated dogs like retrievers may need weekly baths to stop them getting smelly, while short-coated dogs like terriers may not require a wash unless they are muddy or salty.

However, even with regular grooming some breeds are particularly susceptible to skin conditions. Keep a close eye on the condition of your dog's coat and skin when you are brushing and grooming it at home, and get any lumps or bumps, sores, bald or flaky patches seen by a vet. Do likewise if there is a change in behaviour, such as an increase scratching or licking, or if the dog is rubbing its head against things.

Allergies

Itchiness, which can present as your dog licking at their feet, hives, inflamed skin and swelling of parts of the body can be signs of an allergic reaction, either to something the dog has eaten or something in the environment. Signs that your dog is having an allergic reaction are the same as in humans: itchy skin, hives (lumps on the skin, which can get quite large and move around to different parts of the body), or a runny nose. You may see your dog repeatedly scratching or licking part of its body.

Allergies causing skin issues are a major problem for some dogs. Some types of grass are a major cause of itchy skin. Some dogs are highly allergic to kikuyu, which is very common in the north, in warmer areas where there is no frost. As well as making the sensitive skin of their tummy and paws itchy, during spring and summer its spores can also be inhaled and cause respiratory allergies. Many dogs will have an allergic reaction to flea bites, too, which is another reason to keep on top of flea treatment.

Most allergies to food also cause skin reactions, rather than gastro-intestinal upsets like vomiting or diarrhoea (like some people get hives from eating strawberries). It can be quite hard to work out which specific ingredient in the dog's food is causing the reaction, and you may have to go through a process of elimination until symptoms improve. Common food allergies in dogs include proteins such as beef or chicken, wheat (gluten) and soy, and all dogs are largely lactose-intolerant. They may be able to tolerate small amounts of cheese or plain yoghurt, but they shouldn't be given milk to drink.

Talk to your vet about ways to treat the underlying causes of your dog's allergies. If your dog has severe allergies, your vet may recommend the use of a steroid, such as prednisone, which is available as a tablet. There is also a treatment for itchy skin called Apoquel, which can be given as a chewable tablet, and an injectable medication called Cytopoint. Neither of these options is cheap, but if you have a dog with long-term, bad allergic itching, they are worth considering. However, bear in mind your dog might have to be on it for life.

Sea water
Salt water, which is rich in minerals and can aid healing, can be good for dogs' skin, but dried salt on the skin can be an irritant. Give your dog a good rinse if it's been in sea water, especially in places where salt might crust up and irritate the skin, such as where the legs meet the belly, along the tummy and under the collar. Also take notice of any water-quality warnings if you are letting your dog swim or paddle in the sea — playing in contaminated water could give it a tummy upset, or cause any scrapes and scratches to get infected.

'Hot spots'

'Hot spots' or moist dermatitis looks like areas of red, inflamed skin, which can occur anywhere on the body but are often on the neck. The skin under the fur can look wet and is sometimes raised, like a hive. Inflamed patches can start off small but get much larger quite quickly, especially if the dog is scratching, licking or biting the area to get some relief.

Hot spots usually start off from a skin irritation caused by a minor scratch or insect bite, or an allergic reaction, but they can be caused by a dog licking itself excessively through stress or boredom. If the dog continues to scratch or chew the spot and breaks the skin, a secondary infection can develop. Hot spots are not contagious but can spread or grow easily. They are more common in humid weather, during which bacteria can flourish.

Unfortunately, hot spots may not resolve by themselves — you may need to have a vet take a look at them, for antiseptic cleaning and other treatment, possibly including antibiotics. Your dog may have to wear a cone around its neck to stop it from licking the area and irritating it further. The spot should start clearing up after a day or two.

Cones and other options

Most dogs will tolerate wearing an 'Elizabethan collar' or cone around their neck if they have an injury or surgical scar they need to be kept away from, but some absolutely hate it and will freak out if they're made to wear one. You can make a soft collar out of a cut-up pool noodle or try using an inflatable neck pillow instead. Another option is putting clothing, like a child's T-shirt or rash shirt, on the dog so it covers the wound. Our Dalmatian–Staffy cross Peggy, who was mostly white, used to wear a little rash shirt a lot of the time to protect her from getting sunburnt, too.

Ringworm

Ringworm isn't actually a worm; it's a fungal skin disease and can very easily be passed on, both between dogs and from dogs to humans. It can look like a patch of hair loss, a crusty spot or a red lesion. It is most commonly seen on young, elderly and long-haired dogs, and can be caught if your dog has a cut or broken skin, which lets the fungus in.

The vet will make a diagnosis using a UV lamp or taking a scraping from the skin. They may then prescribe a topical medication to rub on the area, and/or an oral medication. Your dog will need to be kept in one part of the house to avoid spreading the spores, and your home will need to be very carefully cleaned. It can be very hard to get rid of, and humans can catch it as well, especially children and older people with weaker immune systems.

When we have a dog with ringworm in the sanctuary or kennels we have to wear special overalls and gumboots when in its enclosure, and make sure to wash and sanitise carefully after contact with them. We just can't afford to have it spread.

Mats and clumps

All dogs need regular brushing or grooming to keep their skin and coat in good condition, but if your dog has long fur or hair you will need to take special care that it does not become matted or clumped. Not only does it look bad, it can also cause skin problems: loose hairs and dead skin cells get caught up in the mat, and bacteria can settle in and cause infections. Mats also cause the skin to be pulled and tightened, weakening it and making it prone to uncomfortable rips and tears. Your dog can become distressed and have trouble moving or sleeping, as the knots catch on things and pull on the tender skin beneath them. It's like having your hair combed when you were a kid — if someone touches or pulls on a knot, the dog's reaction might be to turn and give them a nip.

Mats are most likely to form where there is friction, such as under the legs, around the collar or on the belly. Just like with humans, tangles can form if the dog has wet hair from a bath or swim. Depending on your dog's coat, matting can happen very easily, and some dogs will need to be brushed every day to prevent tangling. If you have a poodle or poodle cross, a bichon frisé, Maltese, shih tzu or another type of 'fluffy', you will need to factor the cost of regular grooming into its care — it will probably rack up more bills at the 'hairdresser' than you do!

Tummy troubles

All dogs at some point will get tummy upsets, which cause vomiting and/or diarrhoea. Sometimes it's from eating too much at once, or eating things they shouldn't — food or otherwise — or from drinking dirty water when out and about. It's not necessarily serious and it can pass quickly, like food poisoning in humans.

If your dog has a bit of diarrhoea — that is, frequent runny poos and less control than usual over when and where it poops — make sure it has access to plenty of fluids so it doesn't become dehydrated. You can also get electrolyte solution from the vet to replace what is being lost through runny poop.

If your dog seems otherwise well, and just vomits once or has one runny poop, it's probably something it ate, and its tummy will calm down. Again, though, do ensure it has access to lots of water, and be proactive about encouraging your dog to drink. A bland diet of boiled chicken and plain rice will help it to settle, too, if it's nothing serious.

Doggy broth

You can make a nutritious broth for your dog to drink while its tummy is upset. Boil up some chicken bones in water — not too much water, to keep the broth dense. Simmer for an hour or so, then strain the liquid, discarding the bones but retaining any fatty or marrow bits. Chill the broth and let it develop a jelly-like consistency. Some people also add apple cider vinegar when boiling the bones, as this helps to draw the goodness out of them.

However, if the diarrhoea doesn't settle down in a couple of days, take the dog to the vet to be checked out, in case the upset is being caused by a parasite (such as giardia), or a bacterial infection like *Campylobacter* or *Cryptosporidium*. It might sound disgusting, but it will be really helpful to the vet if you can take along a poop sample for analysis.

The same applies for vomiting, you should be able to see kibble shapes (or whatever else it has been eating). It could just be 'dietary indiscretion' causing the problem, in which case the dog will probably perk up after having a wee chuck. But if your dog is vomiting repeatedly and forcefully and seems generally unwell, it could be a sign of a more serious disease, such as parvo, or even bloat (see page 214). Repeated vomiting can also lead to dehydration. If there is any blood in the vomit, take your dog to the vet immediately. Take a photo of the vomit, or — brace yourself — scoop some up in a zip-lock bag to show to the vet, who might be able to diagnose what is wrong from looking at the consistency and colour. If a dog is vomiting frequently and has stopped eating, get in touch with your vet as soon as possible.

This is especially true with puppies. There are some nasty bugs out there that can kill young dogs, so seek advice as soon as possible. For adult dogs, it depends what's happening: if your dog is quiet or crying, with diarrhoea and vomiting, take it straight to the vet.

Some dogs, like some children, have a sensitive stomach and are just habitual chuckers. In this case you might need to investigate special foods that agree with your dog's digestive system. Sometimes this intolerance can be caused by allergies to certain food ingredients, such as grains or beef. Our big boy, St Bernard Jeffrey, is on a special diet with a fish-based kibble with no grains. Considering he eats ten to twelve cups of kibble a day, it can get quite expensive; but picking up after a St Bernard with a tummy upset is no fun, we can tell you!

Eating things they shouldn't

Dogs can also vomit if they've eaten something they shouldn't. This is just a dog thing! Dogs love to chew and explore things with their mouth. That means they will ingest all sorts of odd things, given half a chance: rocks, pieces of clothing, coins . . . you name it, a dog's probably tried eating it. Unfortunately, that also often means items that can be harmful to them, such as socks, batteries, foods which are toxic to them, and objects that can cause intestinal blockages.

The best way to deal with this is environmental control: try to ensure there are not things lying around which your dog shouldn't eat. Supervise their play and chewing, to make sure parts of toys don't get eaten. Don't

let them eat things from the rubbish or compost, such as fruit stones or corncobs. It's not only solid objects that cause trouble — string, rubber bands, ribbons, sweetcorn husks, plastic bags and bits of rope can also cause huge problems if they get tangled up as they pass through.

Most dogs also can't help themselves eating disgusting things they come across at the park or at the beach, and will have a chomp on dead birds or rotting fish given half a chance, so keep an eye on them when out and about.

Another thing to keep an eye out for, if you take your dog to the beach, is poisonous sea slugs. Some types contain a substance called tetrodotoxin, which is poisonous to dogs (it can also cause nausea and numbness in humans). If you think your dog might have eaten or even licked one, contact your vet immediately. Similarly, pufferfish sometimes wash up on New Zealand beaches, and these, too, contain tetrodotoxin. The poison is so powerful that some dogs that have ingested it don't even survive getting off the beach.

Dogs may also be exposed to toxins in the environment, through eating poisonous plants or coming into contact with other toxic substances, such as bleach, rat poison, slug baits or spray-on exterior cleaning products. They may walk on something poisonous and then lick it off their paws. If they are particularly thirsty they may drink dirty water, or be exposed to *E. coli* and other bacteria through swimming or playing in water that has been contaminated with sewage.

If your dog has eaten something it shouldn't, the item or substance may pass through the digestive tract and out the other end. However, if you suspect your dog is unwell after eating something odd, or poisonous, contact the vet immediately. In many cases surgery will be required to remove the object and save the dog's life. Once again, prevention is much better than cure!

Constipation — or diarrhoea?

If your dog is straining as if it wants to poop but nothing is coming out, it could be a sign of diarrhoea and an upset tummy, rather than constipation. Talk to your vet about the best treatment.

Bloat/stomach flips

If you have a large dog, with a big chest and small waist, they are at greater risk of getting a very dangerous condition called stomach flips, twisted gut, bloat or, more technically, gastric dilatation–volvulus (GDV). This occurs when a dog's stomach fills with gas, food or fluid and basically turns over on itself internally. It develops without warning, can progress quickly and should always be treated as a medical emergency — a dog can die in an hour or two without treatment.

Surgery is the only solution if the stomach has flipped, but the good news is that, while the vet is reversing the flip, they can also sometimes fix the organ in place internally so it can't flip again. The fixing surgery can also be done preventatively.

If your dog's breed is susceptible to flips, it's very important that these dogs should not eat too fast or drink too fast. Signs to look out for are the dog seeming restless or agitated, a swollen tummy (as gases build up internally), drooling or panting, and eventually being unable to stand. While larger, big-chested dogs are most at risk, it can happen to any dog, so be aware of it and take action if you have any concerns.

One of our dogs, a mastiff–pit bull cross called Bella, had a bloat attack and they had to puncture her abdomen to let the gas out. They then gave her the surgery to stop the stomach from flipping again, but it happened anyway. Fortunately, she survived, but we stopped adding up the cost of her treatment when it rose above $12,000. In this case we didn't have insurance because of her age, so we just had to find the money.

So with big dogs, it is best not to feed them in one go, in case they give themselves bloat (see feeding, chapter 6).

Anal glands

It's an unfortunate fact of dog ownership that sometimes a dog's anal glands can get blocked. This can lead to infection and abscesses and the dog becoming very unwell.

The anal glands are positioned near the dog's rectum. When the dog pushes out some poop, it presses on the glands and adds a little bit of strong-smelling fluid that acts as the dog's 'business card'. This is what dogs are smelling when they sniff each other's bottoms in greeting, and also when they sniff other dogs' poop. If the poop coming out is not firm enough to stimulate the glands, they can become full, and the fluid can become thick and block the exit to the glands, causing irritation, infection and possibly impaction.

You'll know if this is happening because of the incredibly bad smell coming from your pooch's behind — a bit like very old, dead fish. They may also be 'scooting' their bum on the ground, and licking or biting their bum.

Problems with the anal gland are more common in small-dog breeds such as toy and miniature poodles, chihuahuas and beagles. Most dogs that are of a healthy weight, get plenty of exercise and are fed a diet containing fibre won't have any trouble with their anal glands, thank goodness.

If your dog is not pooping firmly enough and the glands are getting blocked, the first thing to do is add more fibre to its diet. One simple way is to give it a bit of Weet-Bix (if the dog is not allergic to wheat) or grated carrot. If the glands become blocked, you will need to take the dog to the vet to have them expressed. Some groomers will also provide this service. If it is a regular occurrence, you may also be able to learn to do it yourself, but it does involve sticking your finger up your dog's bottom.

Foot problems

Issues can occur with the tender pads of the feet if the dog stands on something sharp or rough or if grass seeds get wedged under the skin. Inspect your dog's paws carefully after you have been walking in long grasses where a seed or spiky bit of grass might have got wedged into the paw pad, or between the toes. If a seed does become wedged under the skin and is irritated or infected, it will need to be cut out by a vet.

The pads of the toes can also get burnt if the dog walks on a hot pavement. This can be very painful and take time and care to resolve, as the blistered skin can peel off and become infected. The best way to avoid this is to never let your dog walk on hot concrete or asphalt. It can be easy to forget how hot the footpath or road is when you are walking on it wearing shoes! Check the temperature by putting your hand on the hard surface — if you can't bear to touch it for more than ten seconds, it's too hot for your dog to walk on. Putting your bare foot on the concrete is a good guide, too — if you can't stand it, the dog can't either.

Fractured and ingrown toenails

Broken toenails can be very painful for the dog, and they can happen quite easily. Dogs can catch a nail on something in the environment while walking or playing, and split, break or even pull out the nail. There may be bleeding and pain, and the nail bed can become infected. The foot will need to be carefully cleaned and also dressed. If your dog is in pain and there is bleeding, you will need to contact your vet.

Keeping your dog's nails short and blunt will help prevent them catching on things and tearing, and from becoming ingrown. For many dogs, walking on hard surfaces like pavement will keep them worn down, but you will probably still have to trim the dewclaws (the extra claws above the dog's 'ankle', which don't touch the ground unless the dog is running). Some dogs absolutely hate having their nails clipped, and you may have to get a groomer or the vet to do the job.

Ingrown toenails are very painful (for dogs and humans!) and may cause your dog to alter its walking or running gait to avoid pain, which in turn can cause muscle and joint injuries. It's a good idea to get your dog used to the idea of having its paws handled and its nails clipped from an early age, so it doesn't become anxious about the process when it's older.

Ear problems

Ear infections are common, especially in breeds with floppy or furry ears and in humid conditions. It can get very warm and damp inside a dog's ear, and bacteria can breed easily. One of the most obvious symptoms of an ear infection is the dog shaking its head or scratching its ears, but there may also be discharge or visible swelling and redness in the ear.

Check your dog's ears regularly and make sure they are clean inside and not gunky. Try not to get water inside them if your dog is being washed, and make sure no water stays inside them after a trip to the beach or a river swim. If your dog is prone to infections, your vet will be able to advise you on how to clean them safely without risking forcing debris or water into the ear canal.

Eye problems

Dogs communicate so much with their big puppy eyes, so it's important to keep them healthy and in good condition. Dogs can accidentally scratch their own eyes with their nails, or scratch them on sticks or get dirt in them when playing outside. If your dog's eye looks red and painful, or if there is a discharge, get it to the vet.

Dogs can also get conjunctivitis, where there is a gummy or crusty discharge (especially after they have been asleep) and the white part of the eye will look pink. This can be caused by a bacterial infection, or it may be caused by allergies. Again, talk to your vet.

Older dogs may develop cataracts or glaucoma, which can affect their vision. With their excellent hearing and sense of smell, most dogs can cope with reduced sight, and even blindness, but it may make them more reactive or snappy if they get a fright from something unexpected.

As noted earlier, some breeds have a particular tendency to develop hereditary eye conditions such as cherry eye and entropion. In cherry eye, the third eyelid gland pops out onto the white part of the eye and has to be surgically corrected by a vet. This condition is most common in mastiffs and other bull breeds, as well as Great Danes, cocker spaniels and shar peis. Entropion is a condition in which the eyelids roll inwards and the lashes can scrape the surface of the cornea, potentially leading to abrasions and corneal ulcers. It is most commonly seen in young pups; an affected dog may hold the eye shut, or there may be a sticky discharge. The remedy, again, is surgical correction.

Dental problems

Dental disease is one of the most common issues for dogs. Even little dogs have lots of teeth — adult dogs have 42, compared to our 32 — and big dogs obviously have very big ones! Teeth can get broken and gums injured when the dog chews or bites hard objects. Tartar can also build up on the dog's teeth and irritate the gums.

Like other carnivores, dogs have smaller incisors at the front of the mouth for nibbling, four big canines or 'fangs' for puncturing and holding onto things (which makes them so good at tugging games), and premolars and molars at the back for chewing and grinding. Puppies have only twenty-eight teeth, which grow in when they are about two weeks old and drop out at around four to six months of age as the adult teeth emerge. Usually these baby teeth get swallowed with food as they drop out when the dog is eating, but you might find one around the house or stuck in a chew toy!

Make a habit of regularly lifting up the jowls and inspecting your dog's teeth and gums to make sure everything looks healthy. It is important that you get to know what your dog's gums look like normally — most dogs have pale or pink gums, but some breeds have naturally dark or spotted gums. The important thing to note is if there are any changes to how they look. Normal gums should look smooth, wet and shiny, and there should be no red patches or bleeding.

If you see anything that looks out of the ordinary or concerning, make an appointment with your vet. It can be quite hard to have a good look inside a dog's mouth, especially if it doesn't like being handled this way, and you don't want to accidentally lose a fingertip!

Oral warts

Young dogs, with their immature immune systems, can develop warts around the mouth and lips, or even inside the mouth and on the tongue. These look a bit yucky but are usually harmless, and disappear on their own without treatment. They are caused by a virus passed on by other dogs, but they're not contagious to humans. They are grey or flesh-coloured and look like tiny cauliflowers, and your dog may get one or several at a time.

Common injuries

Again, dogs are like humans — sometimes they can overdo it with physical activity, and pull or injure a muscle or joint. Dogs aren't very good at making decisions about what they're physically capable of, so it's up to you as the

owner to make sure they don't accidentally injure themselves playing or running.

Insect stings

Dogs spending time outdoors, especially in grass, can get stung by bees, wasps and other insects. They can be quite fascinated by this thing buzzing around them, and might even eat a 'spicy sky raisin', which can cause their mouth and throat to swell. They might also accidentally stand on a bee or wasp.

Most dogs recover quite quickly from a bee or wasp sting, with irritation and pain lasting only a few hours, but some can have an allergic reaction. If your dog starts to struggle to breathe; if its mouth, throat, neck or head swells up; or if it collapses after being stung, contact the emergency vet urgently. Otherwise, make sure the sting is no longer in the dog, wash the area, and apply a cold pack if your dog will tolerate it, to minimise discomfort and swelling.

Bite wounds, cuts and scratches

If your dog has been in an altercation with another dog and suffered a bite, it needs to go to the vet. It may need stitches, and definitely some antibiotics to prevent infection. You probably won't know anything about the other dog, and the bacteria in dogs' mouths mean their bites are really germy. It can also be hard sometimes to see the full extent of a bite wound, particularly if your dog has long hair, so it's best to have the vet check it and shave the area to see if it needs stitching.

Bite wounds, and other cuts and scratches, can develop into painful abscesses if they become infected. Keep an eye out for the area around the wound becoming red or feeling warm to touch. The pus filling the abscess may need to be drained by the vet, and your dog will need antibiotics to fight the infection.

Minor cuts and scratches should heal on their own; just keep the area clean and keep an eye on it to make sure it is coming right. Talk to your vet if you have any concerns.

Fractures

Your dog may break a bone if it has a fall, lands awkwardly or is hit by a vehicle. The most commonly broken bones are in the legs, especially the hind legs, but the pelvis and jaw can also be broken in a bad accident. As with human bones, fractures can be partial, complete and/or open (when the bone is exposed through the skin).

If you suspect your dog has any kind of fracture, get it to the emergency vet immediately. Many breaks can heal completely with the correct treatment and rest, but it is important to follow the vet's advice closely to make sure the break is fully repaired and there are not any ongoing problems.

Muscle, ligament and skeletal problems

Because of the relatively small gene pool in New Zealand, lots of dogs here seem to have a genetic disposition to ligament damage. Only working and racing dog breeds seem to be largely free from it. There seems to be an inherited weakness that makes it more likely that a dog will injure a ligament — like the cruciate ligament which holds their knee together. The ligament can tear or snap entirely if the dog skids, twists or turns, or jumps and lands awkwardly. Some vets believe these ligaments are more likely to be weak if the dog has been desexed too young, but there is evidence on both sides of this (and you know our position on desexing as early as possible!).

Symptoms of cruciate ligament damage range from your dog limping a little to not being able to bear weight on the leg at all. If your dog seems to be walking in an unusual way, favouring a leg or having trouble getting up and lying down, this could be the problem — talk to your vet. Your dog may need surgery to fix the problem, although with smaller dogs and less severe tears the ligament can repair itself with rest and anti-inflammatory drugs. Surgery to fix the problem is expensive, so once again it's good to have pet insurance.

Unfortunately, once a dog has damaged its cruciate, it can happen again, on the same leg or on the other one, and the dog is likely to develop arthritis later in life (see page 223). Cruciate ligament injuries are also more common in overweight dogs, where extra stress is placed on the joint, so the best thing you can do is keep your dog at a healthy weight and limit any exercise that involves too much jumping or skidding.

You can also help protect your dog's joints by not letting it jump down off surfaces like the sofa, especially when it is young — say, under about eighteen months for larger breeds. (Jumping upwards is not so bad, as the dog is not landing with its full weight behind it.) That's another reason not to let the dog up on the couch or bed, unless you want to lift it down each time! If you have an older or smaller dog and you want it to enjoy cuddles with you on the sofa, you may have to provide a ramp to enable it to climb up and down safely and comfortably.

Puppy bones

When puppies are born, their bones are almost 'floating', joined together by growth plates that are soft cartilage, which hardens into stronger, denser bone as the puppy grows up. Consequently, they can easily damage their joints and ligaments.

Always put a puppy down gently, with all four feet on the ground. Don't drop it, or let it jump down from your arms or lap onto the ground; this could damage the growth plates, resulting in the bones not growing correctly. Puppies' bones are in any case quite weak and can easily fracture. For the same reason, it's really important not to overexercise puppies (see pages 235–236).

Patellar luxation (kneecap dislocation)

Another common condition, mostly seen in smaller dogs, is patellar luxation. In mild cases the kneecap slips out of its usual position briefly as the dog is walking or running, then returns to its rightful place. The dog might limp for a few steps, shake its hindleg or give a little skip, then continue walking as normal. In milder cases, physio and exercises may help, but more severe cases will require surgery to repair the problem. It's also important to keep the dog's weight down, so as little stress is possible as placed on the faulty joint.

Hip dysplasia
This is a genetic condition in which the hip joints develop abnormally, so the ball and socket don't fit together correctly and can become unstable. It's more common in larger dogs, but can occur in any breed. Symptoms usually start to show before the dog is a year old — they may have difficulty going up stairs, walk with an unusual gait, or struggle getting up off the ground. Unfortunately, this condition can't be cured, but it can be managed by weight control, careful exercise and possibly surgery. A dog with hip dysplasia can still live a long and happy life.

Broken wag

Did you know that dogs can sprain their tail from wagging it too hard or swimming too much? It's known as 'limber tail' or 'broken wag', and it can be quite painful for the dog.

A dog with broken wag will have a limp tail or hold it pointing downwards. The dog will avoid moving it, and the area where it joins to the body will be sensitive to touch. It's upsetting for the dog not only from a pain point of view, but also because the dog cannot use its tail to communicate. Fortunately, most tail sprains come right with rest, although the vet may prescribe anti-inflammatories.

Arthritis
Just like humans, older dogs may develop osteoarthritis when the cartilage that cushions their joints has worn away. Your dog will start being a bit 'creaky' — stiff after exercise or on waking, maybe limping, being reluctant to climb stairs or jump. Again, there is no cure, but the condition can be managed, especially by keeping your dog's weight at a healthy level (see pages 171–173).

Ash is a tattoo artist based in Warkworth, north of Auckland. She adopted Ralph (originally Jack) from the 'Alcohol' litter in 2020.

We had family dogs in my teenage years, but they were smaller — chihuahua crosses. I always wanted a dog of my own. My uncle had Rottweilers when I was growing up and I adored them, but my parents always said I wasn't allowed my own dog until I was responsible enough — something I understand now.

    I was working making coffee on a Saturday morning, and one of my customers suggested I get in touch with Helen and Gavin and start volunteering at the sanctuary. I lasted three months before I met Ralph, then eight weeks later we became roommates.

    I was there the day the puppies were surrendered — Ralph and ten of his siblings in a cardboard box. Because I was there when they arrived, I got quite attached to them and started coming in every day and hanging out with them. Ralph would always sit at my feet while waiting for his food. He had the darkest coat of all the puppies, with bright blue eyes, and I loved that — he was a little different to all the others.

    We think his mother was a shar pei–Labrador cross, and there seems to be a bit of pittie or Staffy in him, and maybe some kelpie. We had no idea what size he was going to be, but I'm really happy with how he's turned out — I was hoping he would be about this size or smaller; not massive, but I wanted him to be able to play like a bigger dog.

It's always been Ralph and me. For the first two years of his life we lived together, just me and him, and I feel we really formed a bond — it was like he kind of chose me, and the timing was right.

Ralph is a great dog. He is kind and sensitive and very smoochy. His energy levels perfectly match mine, and we have grown together. He definitely has his quirks. Dog puberty was challenging — he had a lot of excess energy and loved the way feather pillows looked inside out. Thankfully he grew out of that phase and into himself.

He gets very nervous around fireworks season, but we are working on being brave. And sometimes he has a funny tummy, so it's appropriate that he's named 'Ralph'. Luckily for us, Helen and Gavin found a great food that works for him.

Ralph has also been fortunate enough to spend a lot of time visiting Country Retreat, and he absolutely adores everyone there. We now live with Kayley, who manages the boarding kennels at Country Retreat, so Ralph is very happy with the extra love he gets there.

When I started volunteering at Country Retreat, I really got an understanding of what happens to unwanted puppies and how many there are that need homes. I couldn't believe the number of puppies being rescued and surrendered. Helen and Gavin are amazing people and incredible at what they do. Thanks to them, there are a lot of happy dogs and people out there.

I love Ralph so much, he is my best friend. Having a dog is one of the coolest experiences in my life so far — I wouldn't change a thing!

8

Keeping your dog happy

Looking after your dog's physical well-being is a high priority, but you don't just want a healthy dog — you want it to be happy as well. Through domesticating dogs, we have taken away their need to hunt for food and the physical and mental challenges that provided, so it is up to us as responsible owners to supply our dogs with adequate physical and mental exercise, as well as food and lots of love. Dogs need both their body and brain exercised to prevent them from becoming bored and potentially destructive or anxious.

A happy dog is a well-behaved dog — and by happy, I don't mean spoilt. I mean that a dog that is having its physical and psychological needs met, with good food, a comfortable home, love and affection — and boundaries — will feel safe and secure. A bit like children, dogs like to know where they stand, and what they can and can't do. If you are able to fulfil your dog's needs — which includes monitoring and, if necessary, modifying how it acts — it is less likely to develop problem behaviours.

Having a well-behaved dog doesn't mean it has to be highly trained, either. It just needs to have basic manners, and know how to behave with other dogs and with people. That means politely greeting other dogs, playing nicely without displaying aggression (or, if it's not a social dog, just ignoring other dogs), not jumping up and running around excitedly when you come home or visitors arrive, and sitting or lying calmly when not being given attention, rather than demanding interaction. By setting clear boundaries from day one, you can teach your dog how you want it to act. It will want to please you; it just needs you to tell it exactly how it can do that.

Dogs like routines, and have a really good sense of what happens in their normal day. If they are usually walked first thing, they will expect that to happen, and get a bit angsty if you change it up! Likewise, they know when meal-times are, and when it's bedtime. Dogs do best in a consistent environment without too many surprises and changes to their routine.

A lot of undesirable behaviour in dogs is caused by either anxiety or boredom. Both of these things can be dealt with, and the dog's behaviour will improve. However, more ingrained behaviours like aggression or reactivity (reacting negatively to other dogs, people, objects or situations) is harder to work with and will probably require the services of a professional trainer (see page 241).

We do a lot of work with the dogs at the sanctuary before we advertise them for rehoming. It's not what you might think of as 'training': often they just need to be taught how to be around both people and other dogs, and to have those basic good manners. Some of the rescue dogs we get are initially very scared and wary of humans, and it can take time before I have built up enough trust to even enter their enclosure or touch them. Then it could take months of patient handling and positive reinforcement before we feel they are ready to go to a new home.

There are a few basic things you need to do to keep your dog happy and settled. As well as food and a comfortable living environment, it will also need regular physical and mental exercise, and those all-important behavioural boundaries. Every dog is different, and you will get to know your own dog's individual personality and needs over time, and how it communicates those to you.

Exercise

All dogs need daily physical activity, such as walks or vigorous playtime, to keep their body fit and their brain stimulated. A dog will let you know if it's not getting the exercise and stimulation it needs — it might be restless, constantly seek attention or bark a lot, and some dogs, especially young ones, may exhibit destructive behaviour if they're not given appropriate outlets for their energy. Not giving your dog adequate exercise may also lead to weight problems and associated health issues (see pages 171–177).

Exercise isn't a one-size-fits-all deal in the dog world: it's all about energy levels and the age and the breed of your fur-baby. Working dogs such as collies and retrievers, and energetic terriers like Staffies, usually need more exercise than the average dog. The breed of dog you choose can be the difference between 'Oh, we're going for a leisurely stroll' and 'Oh no, we've just entered the zoomy zone!'

We've had people say, 'I want a small dog because I only want to do short walks.' But be warned: some small dogs have a lot of energy. Jack Russells and fox terriers will have you playing fetch till your arm falls off. If you're not up for marathon walks, you're actually better off getting a big dog with a massive body, like a mastiff. Take them out for a quick fifteen to twenty minutes around the block and they'll look at you like, 'All right, I'm ready for a nap now.'

Most adult dogs need between thirty and sixty minutes of exercise a day, which can be split into two blocks. For small to medium-sized dogs with relatively short legs, a half-hour walk will make them feel like they've covered a lot of ground, and they will be happy to flop down for a nap afterwards. I'd recommend walking your dog in the morning, when it is fresh and full of energy (and it's not too hot in summer), then let it have a rest. In the afternoon, unleash the fun in your backyard, do some training or playing fetch, and exercise your dog's brilliant mind. In the evening, take it for another stroll — it's a dog's version of a night out on the town.

Senior dogs will need less exercise. Be careful, too, not to overdo it with puppies: though they may seem like little balls of energy, young puppies don't actually need to be walked at all — and in fact, exercising them on a hard surface can be bad for them, as their bones are still very soft and their joints are still developing. A rough rule of thumb is to walk them for no more than five minutes for every month of age: so ten minutes or so when they are two months old, then half an hour by six months. They will get most of the exercise they need just tearing around, playing and being puppies at this early stage. As noted earlier, it's also important not to let your pups and young dogs jump off things, as it can cause a lot of damage to their little bones and joints.

When you're out walking your dog, remember that for them it's not just a matter of going from A to B, or trying to get around a circuit as quickly as possible. A big part of the walk for the dog is the mental stimulation provided by experiencing the environment and having a good sniff. Smell is the dog's primary and most powerful sense — it can identify smells at least a thousand times better than we can, due to the hundreds of millions of olfactory receptors in its nose. Using this incredible sense of smell, your dog can get up to date on what other dogs have been in the area (and have peed on various things), and what other animals and humans have been up to. You need to allow your dog plenty of opportunities to sniff when out walking, but make sure it knows you are in charge: it can't just stop every few paces and sniff everything. Reward it for responding to a 'leave it' or 'walk on' command (see pages 244–253).

Some people like to run with their dogs, and that can be OK as long as the dog is physically capable and enjoys it. Some hunting breeds, like Weimaraners, pointers and vizslas, may be able to run for a decent distance, but most dogs are more into sprint-and-drop. You will need to build up your dog's stamina and be sure it's not overdoing it. I would not advise running with a dog under eighteen months old.

If your schedule doesn't permit you to exercise your dog as much as it needs, you may need to pay for a dog walker in your neighbourhood or for your dog to go further afield on a more adventurous pack walk now and then. Just do your homework on who you're entrusting your dog to; you don't want your pup coming back with a PhD in mischief and lots of bad habits it's been allowed to pick up from other dogs.

Sniffing

- While all dogs are super smellers, some breeds can detect scents better than others. It makes sense that long-nosed dogs are able to distinguish scents better than short-faced ones, and dog types that have been bred to sniff out prey, like the bloodhound, have the best scent-detection abilities of all dogs. Gundogs like retrievers and spaniels, which were originally bred to fetch game, are particularly enthusiastic sniffers when out on walks.

- Dogs sniff people to gather information about us and where we've been, and sometimes the state of our health and emotions. Sometimes they can sniff us from a distance to get the data they need, but some dogs like to get up close and personal, shoving their face into your crotch to get close to where your scent is most concentrated.

- Dogs sniff each other's bottoms for the same reason: there is a lot of information that can be gathered from sniffing around the anus and genitals. Dogs need to be taught how to greet other dogs politely (see page 245–248), sniffing its face first, not just going straight for the bum.

- After sniffing something, your dog may pee on it, to leave its own mark. Think of this as returning a 'pee-mail' left by another dog.

Games and toys

Playing with your dog is another way to provide physical exercise and mental stimulation, as well as giving it something constructive (rather than destructive) to do when you're not around or it needs to entertain itself. I like to make or buy toys that will make the dog think and give it a challenge. Some working breeds, such as collies, need a huge amount of mental stimulation so they don't become bored and start behaving in undesirable ways, including excessive chewing and barking. We get people who call up the sanctuary and say they can't handle their dog any more because it's barking and running around all the time, or it's chewing and destroying things. But you can't blame the dog — it's going to make its own fun if you don't give it enough.

This doesn't mean you have to play with it and entertain it all the time; a five- or ten-minute burst of play or training a few times a day, and one or two walks around the neighbourhood to check out what's going on outside the house, should satisfy most dogs and make them happily tired and adequately stimulated.

What toys your dog will like most will depend on its breed, temperament and personality. Scrappy little dogs like terriers love tug and rope toys — they love a bit of controlled rough-and-tumble, tug-of-war, being play-chased, or chew toys. Other dogs will like toys that make a noise or move erratically, like a Kong or a plastic egg, or cuddling up with soft toys (although some dogs will pull all the stuffing out of them). Most dogs like to play with balls, big or small, and other objects that can be thrown and retrieved, like Frisbees or soft flying discs. A round of throw and fetch is not only good physical exercise, but can also challenge the dog, if you mix up how you throw and keep the dog on its toes.

Toys and games work best when they are tied to dogs' natural instincts: to retrieve, sniff out, chew and lick, capture, destuff. They also want to please you and be praised, and love interacting and playing with you, reinforcing your bond.

Entertainment ideas

Here are some more ideas for challenges and brain games you can set up for your dog.

- Before you head off for a few hours, go out into the garden and hide treats for your dog to hunt down.

- Turn an old muffin tin into a fun puzzle by placing treats in some of the cups and covering them with tennis balls, encouraging your dog to use its problem-solving skills to retrieve the treats.

- Put treats or kibble inside an old tennis ball with a hole or slit in it, big enough for the kibble to fall out, but they have to work for it. Likewise, pack a Kong toy with treats or kibble and seal it with peanut butter — or, for a longer-lasting challenge, freeze it with plain unsweetened yoghurt, peanut butter or other treats inside. (Make sure you use a peanut butter without Xylitol, as this is toxic to dogs.) Kongs and balls are good because they move around and the dog has to concentrate on keeping them still and manipulating them to get the food out.

- You can also put treats or kibble into a plastic bottle, such as a small- to medium-sized soft drink or milk bottle (throw the lid away, as it's a choking hazard), and let the dog work on trying to get the kibble out. Dogs love the crackliness of the bottle as they chew it. Another option is to wrap treats in an old towel and tie it in knots so they have to gnaw away to get the food out, or ball up some old socks with kibble inside.

- Use a LickiMat or make something similar of your own at home. These are a silicone shape with a raised surface which you spread with a food that has to be thoroughly licked off. Toppings can include peanut butter, plain yoghurt, cooked mashed pumpkin or kūmara, cottage cheese, raw egg, mince, mashed banana, wet dog food or dog roll. You can freeze the mat first to make it last longer and be cooling on hot days. Licking like this helps dogs calm down and regulate anxiety and stress, as well as giving them a challenge and a chance to engage their senses. You can also spread the food on a silicone ice cube tray or baking sheet.

- In summer, freeze treats inside a block of ice in a margarine or ice cream container (depending on the size of your dog). Your dog can spend ages pushing the ice block around outside, chewing it and waiting for it to melt so it can get at the goodies inside.

Hide treats or spread a bit of peanut butter inside a cardboard box or tube, then tape up the lid or ends. Your dog will be fascinated by the rattling sound and motivated by the smell of food to try to get the treats out.

Look on YouTube or Google and you'll find lots of other ideas for homemade dog toys — you don't have to spend lots of money on expensive knick-knacks that are just going to get chewed to bits. Just make sure that the materials you are using are safe, and take the toy away when it gets to the stage where pieces might get swallowed — for example, once the dog has pretty much destroyed the plastic bottle, or the towel or sock is reduced to threads that might get ingested and cause digestive problems. Puppies in particular have a natural urge to explore and chew, which means toys can sometimes take a beating. To be both practical and budget-friendly, look for dog toys at second-hand and charity shops.

Another way to keep your dog's brain sharp and engaged is to do a bit of training every day. It doesn't have to be anything complicated — just reinforce skills your dog already has, like come, sit and stay, or teach it something new. Even if you feel like your dog is well trained, it's still good to run through the basics, like sit, down, stay, come, and so on, rewarding it with treats. The dog gets to exercise its brain and gain the satisfaction of succeeding.

Training

Being consistent with rules and boundaries will teach your dog what basic behaviour is expected of it. You can then work on getting it to respond to commands — and teaching it tricks, if you want. If you want to go beyond the basics, or you feel like you need support to teach your dog to behave properly, there are lots of dog trainers out there: just do your research on their methods and talk to other dog owners about their experiences.

You don't need to teach your dog to beg or dance or roll over on command, but you do need your dog to have basic manners: to know how to greet other dogs and people; to not jump up; to sit down on command, and stay there; to leave objects alone, not just chew and eat whatever it wants; and to calm down or go to its bed when you need space. For me, a dog is 'well trained' if it comes when it's called, sits on command, greets people and other dogs nicely and doesn't jump up. If you then want to teach it special tricks, go for it — but get those basics down first.

I'd also like to say here that I'm not a dog trainer. A lot of my opinions and techniques have been developed just from a combination of my experience and common sense. I'm lucky enough to be able to read dogs quite easily, most of the time, which helps to work with them. But all dogs are individuals, and therefore I can't offer any one-size-fits-all advice on training and behaviour management.

Socialisation

Socialisation is very important for all dogs, but especially puppies. This doesn't just mean hanging out with other dogs: it means being exposed to a range of different people, places, smells, sounds and experiences during the formative early months of its life, so it can grow into a confident, happy dog with no major fears or anxieties. Because they are a pack animal, most dogs like to be around other dogs and people — and may have a preference for one or the other — although some dogs are simply less social than others.

Once your puppy has had its first set of vaccinations, at around eight weeks, you can enrol it in a local puppy school. These are good for socialisation for puppies and owners, as you will meet people with dogs at around the same age and stage, and can share experiences and advice. Make sure you choose one that is held in a safe, clean area like a vet clinic, rather than someone's backyard, so your dog will be less likely to pick up any diseases. These classes are often run by vet nurses or experienced trainers, so you will get lots of good health and behavioural advice. We still take puppies along to them and often find out new ways of doing things.

If you have adopted an adult dog, it may have been inadequately socialised when young (especially if it was a Covid puppy that spent a lot of time at home during lockdown), and may have developed some fears or anxieties,

which can manifest in aggressive or reactive behaviour. Dogs that are poorly socialised may not know how to greet other dogs properly (see pages 245–248), and may try to dominate or show aggression towards the other dog. They might also not know the 'rules' of play or how to read the body-language cues of other dogs, leading to misunderstandings and potential fights.

You may need the advice of a professional trainer if your dog has major issues, but if they are just a bit apprehensive you can help build their confidence by gently introducing them to new situations, people or dogs by taking them to parks or other public places, visiting friends and family who have dogs, and taking them to obedience classes. Take it slowly, and always observe how your dog is behaving and what that is telling you; if it is really uncomfortable, remove it from the situation before it escalates and your dog gets overwhelmed and reacts badly. It's also important to praise and reward your dog for positive interactions.

Small dogs in particular are very good at acting scared of everything, shaking and appearing to be highly nervous. Some people really humanise that reaction, picking them up and cuddling them to reassure them, but in doing so they are simply reinforcing the behaviour. My advice is to redirect them: call them to you, ask them to sit, and reward them for doing the positive thing. If you act like the world is a scary place, they are going to pick up on that and continue to lack confidence.

Toilet training

If you adopt an adult dog it will usually (although not always) be toilet-trained, and know it needs to go outside if it has to pee or poop. We do get adult dogs at the sanctuary that have never had this training, through neglect or mistreatment, which can be quite an issue, because no one wants their dog going to the toilet inside! We don't have the time or facilities to toilet-train the puppies at the sanctuary, so often this is the first task for owners once they take their new family member home.

While it might take a bit longer for adult dogs with ingrained habits to learn better behaviours, fortunately, toilet-training puppies is reasonably easy, as long as you are patient and consistent. It should take only a couple of weeks of guidance, reminders, praise and rewards for them to get the gist — much quicker than a human baby! A puppy's bladder starts off pretty small and generally needs emptying one hour for every month of age, so by the time you bring your eight- to ten-week-old puppy home it should be able to hold on for around two hours.

You will need to take your dog outside and encourage it to wee every hour or so, as well as when it starts looking like it wants to go — squatting, circling or sniffing around rather than playing or sleeping. Take it outside to the place where you want it to pee and give it a simple command: 'toilet' or 'wee' or whatever. Praise and reward the dog when they get it right, and it should quickly start making the association: when I need to go, I have to come out here and everyone will be happy with me! Take it out first thing in the morning and just before bed, too, so it starts to learn a bit of a routine. And taking it to a regular spot to wee and poop will make clean-up easier later on, otherwise your dog will consider the whole world is its toilet (which it kind of is)!

I'm not a big fan of teaching dogs to wee inside on a puppy pad, because eventually you are going to have to retrain them to go outside anyway by moving the pad outside. Their only real use is if you're crate-training your puppy and you want it to pee on the pad when it's in the crate; even then, most dogs know not to pee on their own bedding, so they will avoid it.

Try to be as relaxed as possible about it, especially if there are accidents: you don't want the puppy to pick up on your stress and associate toileting with anxiety. The old advice of rubbing its nose in it doesn't work — maybe you should rub your own nose in it, for not noticing the dog needed to wee! Instead, if you catch your dog weeing inside, scoop it up, take it to the 'right' spot and reward it for going there instead.

'Polite greeting'

It's important to teach your dog how to greet other dogs 'politely' and appropriately, without being dominant, aggressive or overexcited. It's all about your dog being confident and calm, so it will help if you keep the lead slack, so no tension is transmitted down it from you to the dog.

When introducing their dog to other dogs, some people will let it stand between their legs, which makes the dog view their owner as a security

blanket, and reinforces their anxiety about meeting other dogs. When doing introductions, I recommend standing away from your dog so that it can learn that it is in charge of itself, and won't always look to you for protection and become anxious if you're not around. You want your dog to succeed, but you have to give it the tools to do so.

Also, a lot of people, when they see another dog approaching, pull the lead to bring their dog in close to them (this is called checking). The dog gets the message that something is wrong, that you're worried about something and they need to be on alert. This can result in the dog developing lead-aggression and reacting badly to other dogs it encounters. The same applies if people scoop up their little dogs when they see a larger or 'scary-looking' dog coming: it's telling the little dog that it is right to be frightened.

Instead, let the lead be slack and allow the dogs to sniff each other, if they want to. Dogs will usually want to sniff the other dog's face and around its bottom, and then, once they have the information they need, they can move on. You can also ask your dog to sit, ready to be calmly greeted.

If your dog is less confident around other dogs, ask it to sit behind you, or stand in front of it, so it knows you are in control of the interaction and it doesn't need to protect you. It's OK to say 'Hi, my dog's in training', so the other person knows their dog shouldn't just rush in and dominate the situation.

'Polite greeting' for humans

Most people greet dogs incorrectly, by approaching the dog head-on, which is a sign of dominance in dog language. Then they reach in and go to pat it on the head — another sign of dominance. And we're usually smiling at them, showing our teeth like we're snarling. It's basically like we're saying to the dog 'I'm the boss', and it's no wonder some dogs react badly to this.

If you want to greet a dog in a non-threatening manner, stand beside it and let it stand beside you. Then you can give it a pat under the chin, so you're not coming in from above in a dominant manner.

Don't push your hand into its face for it to sniff — it can already smell you well enough, and you don't want it to feel threatened and give you a nip. Just stand quietly and let it come to you if it wants to say hello.

Basic commands

All dogs need some basic training to make sharing your home with them practical and enjoyable. A dog that is allowed to do whatever it wants and has no boundaries will be a nightmare to live with and may develop undesirable habits, thinking it is the leader of the pack and it can tell you what to do. Your dog also needs to know some basic commands to keep it safe when you're out and about.

It's good to get started on the basics early — puppies are eager to learn, and respond well to positive reinforcement in the way of praise and/or food treats. Most older dogs are also receptive to training: they will be keen to please you, and will look to you for guidance on how to act. Some breeds of dog are considered to be easier to train than others, as they have been bred to follow commands, such as gundog breeds, while others may have a slightly more independent frame of mind, shall we say! Patience and consistency are key when training any dog, as is making sure you're in a positive and relaxed frame of mind when you are trying to teach it something — dogs are very sensitive to human moods and will pick up on any stress or anxiety you are feeling. You want your dog to form a positive association with the behaviours you are trying to teach, not to obey your orders out of fear of being punished.

The basic premise of all training is to reinforce and reward the behaviour that you want, and ignore or redirect any behaviour you don't want. Most dogs respond well to small food treats as rewards, but some also respond to lots of verbal praise, pats and cuddles, or to the opportunity to have extra playtime with you and/or a special toy. You will get to know what motivates your dog.

It's been estimated that most dogs know the meanings of around ninety different words, and super-smart ones can recognise up to 200! But keep your commands simple, and don't bury the key instruction in a sentence —

just one or two words is best.

Another thing to remember is that the dog's name and the command are two separate things: just calling the dog's name over and over without telling it what to do won't give you the result you want. Call the dog's name to get its attention, then give it the command: come, sit, drop it, etc.

I also train by teaching the dog a hand signal first, then adding a voice command. Having your dog respond to hand signals can literally be a lifesaver: if your dog is at a distance from you — for example, if it's on the other side of a road and you need it to stay till you get to it — being able to make a command using a hand signal can be incredibly useful. Likewise, if you are separated in a noisy environment or they are some distance away, being able to recall your dog with a hand signal will save you having to shout. I think teaching your dog hand signals is one of the most important training things you can do.

Name, recall
Dogs are pretty quick to pick up on the fact they have a specific name. Start by saying your dog's name in a cheery voice, then, when it looks at you, reward it with a positive response and a treat. It will soon make the connection, and you will be able to attract its attention from further away. You can then move on to teaching 'come', which is one of the most important skills a dog can have.

Trainers call this 'recall', and it basically means your dog comes to you when you call it. This can take a bit more time and effort, especially once you move beyond the bounds of home and into a more distracting and stimulating environment like the park or the beach, where there are other dogs, people, birds, smells and so on. The aim is to make yourself the most exciting thing to the dog, and the idea of returning to you on command more rewarding than running off and chasing balls or seagulls. It needs to want to come back to you because something nice or fun is going to happen, rather than thinking it is being told off or its fun time is up. Use a cheerful, excited voice and wave your hands, and when they come to you, reward them by having a little play with a pull toy or something else fun, so they think you're a fun person to be with and stay near to.

If you can get your dog's attention by calling its name but then it seems reluctant to give up the interesting thing it is doing and come back to you, you need to make yourself more exciting, and the idea of returning to you more rewarding. Don't walk towards the dog or chase it: that will become another fun and exciting game for the dog — and frustrating for you. Start to walk away, so they want to come and see what you're doing without them.

You can practise using a long lead, so your dog can wander a short distance but still be attached to you, until you get your recall down pat. You can get 10-, 15- or even 20-metre long-lines, so the dog can have plenty of freedom to roam without the risk of them getting away entirely. One of the good things about using a long-line is if they are not listening to coming back to you, you can stand on the line to pull them up short, which will turn their head and return their attention back to you.

Until your dog has absolutely reliable recall — it will come to you every time you call, no matter what — you shouldn't have it off the lead in public places. Your dog needs to be under your control even when it's off-lead, otherwise it might knock over a child or elderly person, get into an argument with another dog, or even run onto the road and get hit by a car. If your dog is not under control, keep it on the lead.

Sit, lie down
Training your dog to sit on command is one of the basics of good dog behaviour. Being able to sit by you and wait for further instructions is an exercise in self-control for the dog, so is a good way to calm it down and get its attention, or cut off any unwanted behaviour like jumping up or begging for attention. The dog learns that sitting quietly is a way to get rewards and extra attention and affection. Being able to sit is also a safety tool — you can ask your dog to sit before you cross the road, or when the front door or the car doors are going to be opened, so it doesn't rush out onto the road.

There are a couple of ways to teach your dog to sit. The way I do it is, I stand up tall, close to the dog, holding up a treat in my hand. The dog will look up at me, and its bottom will move down correspondingly. As soon as it touches the floor, it gets the treat. Once they have learned the movement, then I add in the word. I always retain the hand signal as well. The other

way to teach sit is to hold a treat near its nose and slowly move it up over its head, so the dog raises its head and lowers its bottom. Reward it when it gets to the sitting position.

Start using the word 'sit' as it starts to move, so it associates the word with the movement. Eventually, the dog will learn to sit on command without being given the food, but remember to keep on praising it with a 'good boy/good girl'.

Once your dog can sit, you can teach it to lie down on command. You might find it easier to teach it to lie from standing, not to sit first. Hold the treat down near the floor so the dog has to lie down to get it. It may try a few times to just bend down, but once it lies down fully, reward it for that. Then you can add the command 'down'.

Stay/wait
Once the dog is responding to the 'sit' or 'down' command, you can start working on teaching it to stay. Build up the amount of time the dog can stay still as you back away from it. 'Wait' is another useful command if you are out walking with your dog either on or off the lead and need it to pause.

Some owners also differentiate between the two commands: 'stay' means 'stay there, I will come back to you', and 'wait' means 'wait there until I signal for you to come to me'. Having these two distinct commands can be very useful, especially if you are in an environment where it would be dangerous for the dog to run to you; for example, if there are cars around. It's useful to have different hand signals for these two commands, so you can give them at a distance (see pages 248–249).

No/leave it
This is a useful command for when you want your dog to either not do something, or stop doing what it's already doing! While most training is about reinforcing the positive, 'no' means paying attention to a negative action for a short while as it gets the hang of learning what you want. One way to teach it is to put a treat in your hand, but when the dog goes to sniff or lick at it, say 'no'. Once the dog stops trying and turns away, then reward it — by providing a treat with your other hand. This may take a while for the

puppy or dog to catch on, but it's a very useful command to have.

With 'leave it', put a treat within the dog's reach, on a table top or similar, and tell it to leave it. Once it can resist for a few seconds, reward it — but with a different treat, not the thing it's been told to leave. Hopefully it will learn that there are certain things — toys, socks, other dog's poop — that it needs to leave alone when instructed. This is useful when you're out with your dog and you want it to not sniff at a cat or pick up and eat something on the ground, for example.

It's also helpful to teach 'drop it', for those times when something which should have been left ends up in the mouth!

Problem behaviours
Chewing
It's hard for dogs to know what they are allowed to chew and what they aren't, so you need to make it clear to them. Reinforce the dog when it is playing with or chewing things that are allowed, and remove the things that aren't. Don't make a big fuss and chase it if it is chewing something it shouldn't — it will think that is part of the game, and your attention is the reward. Instead, either calmly instruct the dog to drop or leave the item, and reward it for that; or distract it with another command like 'come' or 'sit', and reward it for responding to the positive command. The most important thing is reinforcing the positive and redirecting the negative behaviour: you're not giving the dog a treat for being bad, you're encouraging it to be good.

Puppies will be extra-chewy when they are teething, as it seems to help soothe the pain and irritation of new teeth breaking through. You might sometimes find a baby tooth which has fallen out or got wedged in a chew toy, but mostly they get swallowed by the dog as it is eating.

An older dog that chews furniture or woodwork like door frames or the edges of decks may be chewing out of boredom or anxiety. Think about what is going on for the dog when it is behaving like this, and take steps to change the situation, instead of punishing the dog. Make sure it has enough things it *can* safely chew. And if your dog seems to have started chewing more than normal, take it to the vet for a dental and health check, in case there is a medical reason behind it or the dog is stressed or in pain.

You can get natural products such as deer antlers or cow hooves for dogs to chew on, but be careful the dog does not damage its teeth on them. I also prefer not to use rawhide or leather-type chews, because if the dog ingests part of them, they can swell in its stomach and cause problems. You want products that will break down and pass through the gut if bits get swallowed. Natural objects, like sticks and pinecones, can splinter and break up when chewed, but you can buy aged olive branches, which are satisfying to chew, and any parts that come off are soft and can pass through the dog's digestive system. Kongs, while clearly not digestible, are nonetheless a good option, as you can put treats inside them and dogs can chew for ages on the firm rubber.

As mentioned earlier, never give dogs cooked bones to chew on; only raw ones. Serious chewers might enjoy gnawing on a cannon bone (the large bones from the legs of cows), but keep an eye on them and remove the bone if it is starting to break up.

Toy training

You can train a dog to recognise its own toys, but you need to be consistent — it's confusing for the dog if it's allowed to chew some socks and not others, or some soft toys but not your child's precious teddy. You can also train it to put its toys away in a box, which is both cute and useful. Tell the dog to bring you certain toys, and give it rewards and high praise when it puts them in the right place.

Jumping up

Many dogs have a natural urge to jump up on their owners and visitors, as a greeting and when they want attention. Again, your goal is to reinforce and reward the positive behaviour — sitting nicely to be greeted, acting calmly — and ignore or redirect the negative (jumping). To get the dog to be calm and focus, you can teach it a 'touch' command, where it comes to you and then 'boops' your hand with its nose. This is a good way to distract and

redirect, making sure the dog is praised and reinforced for being calm and making a connection with you.

Many people unintentionally encourage their dog to jump up by using a higher-pitched voice to greet it and giving it lots of pats and rubs as it jumps around them. Even if you are pushing the dog down and saying 'No', it is still getting feedback and the behaviour is being reinforced. If a dog is jumping up, I turn my back on it without saying anything, and therefore take away the audience for the behaviour. Make yourself boring and the dog will stop jumping up at you. Once it is calm, ask it to sit and give it a treat.

If you don't want your dog running to the door barking and jumping every time someone turns up, start working on this from day one. Anyone who comes through the door — you, your family, any visitors — will need to *not* acknowledge the dog until it comes and sits quietly. Just ignore it until it's quiet and calm, then you can make a fuss and tell it how much you love it. It's like dealing with a toddler having a tantrum: if you ignore the behaviour or walk away, the performance will naturally come to an end.

Carrying treats

If you're out and about with your dog, always have a few treats with you, to reinforce good behaviour. This is especially useful as a distraction, if you have a reactive dog. If you are approaching another dog or some other trigger, you can scatter a few treats on the ground to distract your dog and refocus its attention. It's about being proactive — as you're walking along, keep an eye out for things your dog might react to, and distract and reward your dog *before* it gets triggered. It's too late once it has been set off!

Pulling on the lead

Good leash manners are absolutely essential. Some dogs take naturally to walking on the lead, and others just want to pull their owners along, especially excitable young pups that are always in a hurry to explore everything. If I'm walking a dog and it just wants to have a sniff of something, I let it, but if it starts to pull me down the road, I stand still until it stops pulling and the lead goes slack; then I start again. Sometimes it can take an hour to walk a kilometre doing this if the dog is a keen puller!

Reward the dog with a treat or praise once it is walking nicely. This will distract it and bring its attention back to you, rather than all the exciting things in the world it is in such a rush to get to. The goal is to have the dog looking to you for direction all the time.

To encourage this, when you're out walking, try a series of rapid changes in direction — first a few steps one way along the path, then a few steps back, then back the other way again, and so on. The dog quickly realises it has to pay attention to you and work out where you're going. Using this technique now and then can help you stay 'in charge' on walks.

Separation anxiety

As discussed earlier, dogs can develop problem behaviours if they are suffering from separation anxiety. They need to be taught from an early age that being on their own for short periods is OK, that they are safe, and that you will come back. Start by getting the dog used to being alone for short periods of time (see pages 128–129), then slowly increase the amount. Just being with the dog all the time is not the answer; if you are constantly with the dog and then you absolutely have to leave it for some reason, it will not be able to cope.

Aggression and reactivity

Dogs may take a dislike to certain types of dogs, especially if they have had a negative experience. If your dog is just not very social, that's OK — you can work with that. It's only if it becomes aggressive or highly aroused around other dogs or people that it is considered reactive.

Nervous or anxious dogs are displaying the flight or freeze aspects of the stress response, whereas aggressive dogs are showing the 'fight' response (fear aggression). Some dogs will back away from you, and others will lunge at you, but both reactions usually stem from fear. Reactivity to other dogs is a hard thing to deal with — a dog like this needs an experienced owner and often support from a professional trainer.

Some dogs are naturally more dominant than others, but most aren't aggressive or reactive unless they have developed it as a behaviour over time, usually as a reaction to fear or mistreatment. It can be very hard to retrain an aggressive dog, sometimes the only solution is for the dog to be put down before it hurts another dog or a person. If your dog has not previously been aggressive and starts exhibiting this behaviour, it's also a good idea to talk to your vet, in case it's a reaction to pain or being unwell which is causing this change.

Working with a trainer can help you to identify triggers and reduce your dog's reactivity. In fact, you may find a trainer to be helpful on a number of issues, such as: if you feel your dog is not respecting your authority and obeying commands; issues with leash walking and recall; resource or barrier guarding, where the dog reacts aggressively trying to protect food or objects, or guards a fence, doorway or gate; if it is biting or nipping, barking excessively or being destructive; or if it is having toilet accidents or deliberately marking.

Often, dog trainers don't actually train your dog — instead, they will teach *you* how to train your dog so you are not reinforcing bad behaviour, and can be more confident in working with and helping your pet to behave better. Remember, too, that consulting a trainer doesn't mean that you have failed in some way as a pet parent: in fact, you are trying to do the best for your dog by working to improve your relationship.

Difficult dogs at the sanctuary

Due to the difficulty of retraining dogs with aggressive traits, I try to avoid taking them on (although sometimes they don't display their aggression straight away, and we find out a bit further down the track, once they've had a chance to decompress). I wouldn't rehome an aggressive dog, but I will rehome a nervous dog, although I'll make sure it is going to experienced owners.

One of our greatest successes with a dog that had aggressive tendencies was Pace (see page 68). When she first came in, we couldn't get near her — she would make a lot of noise and act scary, reacting out of fear. Finding the right place and right home for her took a long time, but now she is living happily with one of our volunteers.

People contact me and say they want to surrender their dog because it has chased or attacked their kids or another animal. In those cases I try to find them help through a trainer, rather than take the dog on myself, because if I rehome that dog and it then kills a cat or attacks a child or a sheep, I couldn't live with myself. Sometimes dogs like that just can't be helped, like our first dog in New Zealand, Fern, and they have to be put down for everyone's safety.

Another reason I avoid taking on reactive dogs in the first place is because most of our sanctuary dogs live in a shared environment in the pods, in groups of three to five. I want to take on dogs that have a good chance of finding a new home, and a dog that is reactive is going to be hard to find a home for — after all, what everyone wants is a dog they can take to the park or the beach or up to school.

That said, we do see lots of dogs that are initially anxious or reacting out of fear, and it can take a while to gain their trust. We take the time to read their responses, and avoid pushing them into uncomfortable situations. Sometimes I'll spend hours just sitting outside a dog's kennel, not making eye contact or even looking in its direction, until it stops seeing me as a threat and allows me to approach it. With such dogs, we can't always get rid of all their nervousness, because we often don't know what they went through before coming to us; but with time, many of them get to a stage where they can be adopted.

Obedience and agility

Taking your dog's training to another level through obedience and agility competitions can be a fun bonding experience, and you'll get to meet other like-minded dog owners. Competitive obedience tests your dog's ability to obey commands and perform tasks such as recall, retrieve, stay, walk at heel, and find items by scent. Working dog breeds such as Border collies, golden retrievers and German shepherds often do well at this, as they're naturally intelligent and easy to train, but any dog with the right temperament can be trained up.

Dog agility involves training your dog to complete a course of various obstacles: jumps, tunnels, seesaws and poles to weave through. Doing agility training can be a good way to focus and harness your dog's energy, and builds a bond through teamwork. It is great physical and mental exercise for your dog, and even if you don't want to compete, you can set up a course of your own at home and just have some fun with it. Just remember not to start your dog too young, while its bones and ligaments are still growing — I'd recommend your dog be at least eighteen months old, depending on the breed, to be safe.

Doggy communication — what does a happy dog look like?

Dogs communicate a lot through their behaviour. They can't talk to us, so they have to use body language and their actions to tell us if they are happy or unhappy, excited, bored, stressed, relaxed, tired, sick or scared. Living with a dog, you will get to know how it communicates what it is feeling: once you get to know each other, you will be able to tell what mood it's in, if it's hungry or needs a drink, if it's keen for a walk or a play, needs to go to the toilet, or wants to show you something.

In terms of overall behaviour, a dog that is having its needs met (i.e. is 'happy') will be relaxed and playful. It may sleep a lot, passing out on the floor or couch rather than pacing around on alert. It will follow your instructions, eat well, and be playful, inviting you to interact with it by brining you toys or doing the 'play bow' (front legs and head down, waggy bottom in the air). Happy dogs like to have physical contact with you, and will lean into you when you touch them or come and snuggle up with you when you're sitting on the couch. You might also find your dog has bursts of 'the zoomies', when it runs around like mad in a sudden burst of energy. This is a sign of happiness!

In terms of body language, a happy dog will have a relaxed body, standing easy or lying comfortably. Its facial expression will be soft, maybe with its mouth softly open; the eyes may be partly closed and the ears floppy, not pricked or pulled back. A dog that is nervous or aroused will stand with a tense posture, its ears either pricked forward or pinned back. Lip-licking and yawning are also signs of stress, or the dog may bare its teeth or clamp its jaw shut. If you can see the whites of a dog's eyes, it's a sign of anxiety or stress.

Just because a dog is wagging its tail doesn't mean it's happy — you need to look at the position of the tail and how fast it's moving. Basically, the faster the wag, the more aroused the dog — with positive emotion like happiness or excitement, or a more negative feeling like nervousness. A relaxed dog will make big sweeps of its tail from side to side, like when it's happy to see you. A faster, twitch-like wag of a tail held high indicates a higher level of arousal, like a guard dog on alert.

A dog that is scared or stressed will try to make itself look smaller, cowering down towards the ground. It may even roll onto its back to show submission. If the dog is standing with its weight held forward, it may be just interested in something, or it may also be trying to appear bigger and more dominant.

Don't assume you can automatically read the signals of a strange dog. People love to say, 'I know dogs,' but I often say, 'You don't know this one.'

Dogs also bark as a form of communication, of course, and some breeds bark more than others. They use different barks to send different messages: an alarm bark sounds different to a welcoming or excited bark, for example. Excessive barking can become an issue if the dog is left home alone without adequate stimulation, or if it is being triggered by another dog nearby or people walking past the house.

If your dog has started barking a lot more than usual, it's a good idea to talk to your vet to make sure there isn't a medical issue behind it. Otherwise, if the dog is barking a lot when you are around, work to retrain it by reinforcing an alternative, positive behaviour like coming to you and sitting quietly. If the barking is happening while you are out, make sure it has plenty of toys to stop it from getting bored and that it's had plenty of

exercise to tire it out. It may also be suffering from separation anxiety (see page 257).

Dogs and affection

Some people tend to humanise dogs too much, and that's how problems can occur. Dogs are smart, and they learn how humans behave, and to accept our habits, in exchange for being looked after. They are better at learning human behaviour and communication than we are at learning dog behaviour!

It's worth remembering that cuddling and hugging and kissing your dog, especially on the face, is not a natural behaviour for dogs. They will learn to tolerate it, and maybe even understand that you are showing them affection and love, but many dogs don't like being held closely. Dogs lick and mouth each other on the head to show submission, so they may be confused by you kissing them on the face or snout. You're asking for trouble if you have your face that close to the dog's mouth and it reacts badly!

If your dog puts its paw on you or its head in your lap, or lies so that part of its body is touching you, that's as close as you're going to get to a hug! Licking you can be a sign of affection, but it can also be a sign of submission or appeasement, which is not such a healthy behaviour.

Ages and stages

Like humans, all dogs go through different stages and phases. Having a puppy is very different to having an elderly dog, but there are things to love and look out for at each stage. Having a dog is a commitment for their lifetime, and it's a wonderful journey to go on together.

Puppy
[up to six months]

- 🐾 Basically a baby, learning about the world
- 🐾 Maximum cuteness! Who doesn't love a puppy?
- 🐾 Keep up with vaccinations
- 🐾 Get toilet training sorted
- 🐾 Do plenty of safe socialisation and basic training
- 🐾 Be prepared for lots of chewing as the puppy is teething!

'Teenage' dog
[six to eighteen months / two years]

- 🐾 Lots of energy and enthusiasm
- 🐾 Adult teeth are coming in, so they may need bigger, tougher things to chew
- 🐾 Behaviour may become challenging as they push boundaries and want to be more independent
- 🐾 Reinforce training; be consistent and positive
- 🐾 Keep up socialising your dog and exposing it to new situations
- 🐾 Reduce feeding to two small meals a day by around six months, depending on the breed and the adult size of the dog.

Adult dog
[two to ten years]

- 🐾 Depending on your dog's personality, they may have calmed down a bit, with fewer zoomies and more chill-out time
- 🐾 Keep up reinforcing training, but your dog should know the rules and follow them by now
- 🐾 Needs less stimulation, exercise and socialisation, but don't let your dog get bored
- 🐾 Chewing may reduce (again, depending on your dog)
- 🐾 Some health issues may start to develop as the dog ages.

Senior dog
[ten years plus]

- 🐾 Slowing down and sleeping more
- 🐾 Coat may become thinner and may become grey around the muzzle and eyes
- 🐾 May have creaky joints and be less agile as arthritis develops
- 🐾 May lose some vision or hearing
- 🐾 May eat less and may develop digestive problems. You may need to reduce feeding or change the type of food so it doesn't gain weight. May also need to eat softer food if it develops dental problems or needs tooth extractions
- 🐾 May develop cancer or other diseases, and require more veterinary care
- 🐾 Will need less walking and playing, but still need lots of love and affection
- 🐾 Just like people, older dogs get aches and pains, and may need regular pain medication

- 🐾 Can be calm and mellow, but older dogs with pain may get more cranky and be less tolerant of children or puppy behaviour — keep an eye on them in those situations. If they've got a sore back or joints it may hurt them even to be stroked, so they may seem more touchy or grumpy

- 🐾 Give them lots of love — they won't be with you for much longer and it is your responsibility to make their twilight years as happy as possible.

Andrew and Luna

Luna, a Staffordshire bull terrier–Rottweiler mix, was adopted by Andrew in 2021. Only around ten months old, she was found abandoned in a forest, tied to a tree with her litter of pups next to her on a blanket, and brought to Country Retreat to be nursed back to health before being rehomed.

I've always been a dog person. My godfather was a dog trainer and I always thought I would get a dog once I reached the age when I felt responsible enough to own one, as it's a massive commitment. I wanted to be able to travel or live overseas first, but a couple of years ago I thought the time was right and that this was a sacrifice worth making.

I was originally looking for a Rottweiler — they were always my favourite type of dog. I had started looking at pure-breds, but also rescue dogs. A friend of my partner volunteered at Country Retreat, and she said the owners were amazing people and that we should go look at the dogs up there. Coincidentally, about two weeks after she told us that, we saw a photo of Luna on the Facebook page, so we decided to visit.

To be honest, at that stage I was still fifty–fifty: I didn't quite feel ready. I'd just bought a house, my relationship was pretty new, and it felt like a big commitment. My godfather recommended I start spending time with the dogs and try to understand their personalities — don't just fall in love with the first dog you see, he said. But with Luna, she was the first one we saw, and we simply couldn't walk away. There was a real connection. She was the sweetest thing — the first time we met her, she went to sleep in my arms. We knew she'd had a hard start to life and we wanted to give her a second chance.

She had no animosity towards people, but we've found out she did have a few quirks. She didn't understand dog etiquette and was very nervous when first meeting other dogs. She tends to stalk them and lunge at them. At first, she would lunge at everything: people, cars, visitors at the door — it was pretty full-on. After three or four months, she started to calm down, but she's still not great with other dogs. She's never got into a fight, but she just doesn't know how to act around them and can be a bit intimidating.

Before we got her, for a year or so during lockdown I'd spent lots of time watching training and behaviour videos online. We've done lots of work with her, and while we haven't completely changed her behaviour she has got better, and we can introduce her to other dogs, so long as it is very structured and consistent.

Luna is crate-trained, and she goes to kennels one or two times a week, depending on my work schedule. I didn't like doing that at first, but we had to because at home she'd jump the fence, even though it's 1.8 metres high.

Having a dog has been a hundred times better than I expected. It's absolutely improved our mental well-being, having someone that looks forward to seeing us every single day. We have to walk her, which forces us out of the house whether it's raining or not. I've also really enjoyed the training aspect, all the recall stuff — it really forms a bond.

It's also a good way to meet people — normally you can stand in line at the beach café and no one will talk to you, but when we have Luna with us we have conversations with ten different people.

It saddens us how people tend to react to Rottweilers. When we first got her, my girlfriend's family were nervous, but now they love her more than anyone. It's the same with a lot of our friends, who initially were worried about our dog, but she wins them over — so we're breaking down that stigma. It's pretty clear, having a dog, that dogs need people. They create such a special bond with humans, yet you see so many dogs in the shelters sitting there by themselves.

Helen and Gavin are doing the most amazing job and they need to be championed. They give so selflessly to these dogs, especially seeing the state of some of the animals when they arrive. I've tried to talk a lot of people into volunteering there!

All dogs can be hard work, but rescue dogs have extra little challenges. Every now and then I think, 'Was this the right decision?' We can meet ten dogs and with nine she's absolutely fine, but one dog can make her a bit tense. I think, 'This is hard, and it's adding stress to my life.' But 99 per cent of the time it's worth it.

It's crazy to think how you can transform the life of an animal. We've given Luna a whole new life.

Helen says:

Luna, once known as Petal, arrived at our sanctuary with her eyes telling a story of abandonment and hardship. With her, she brought seven fragile little puppies. At just four weeks old, her pups were not just hungry, but also infested with fleas, ticks and worms. Luna, despite her youth and suffering, had fiercely protected them, but once they were brought to safety, her demeanour changed, and she started to reject her own litter.

In the face of her aggression, we made the difficult decision to separate Luna from her pups, enabling us to hand-raise them with the care they deserved. Then Luna's own transformation could begin.

It was a challenge to get Luna to understand she was safe and that no one was going to hurt her. When we have dogs that show any sign of aggression, only Gavin and I handle them, as we don't ever want to risk the safety of our volunteers. I would sit for hours in the same room as her, throwing treats so she could pick them up, and talking gently to her. Her growls lessened, and one day a huge breakthrough came when she finally sat next to me. It's at moments like this that I remember why I do what I do! Luna had started to trust me. It was almost like a switch had been thrown — her demeanour changed further, and she soon became a smoocher with so much love to give.

With every bit of love, nourishing food and gentle care, Luna bloomed into a stunning, vibrant young dog. Her spirit mended and her trust in humanity was restored.

Emma adopted mixed-breed Otis in 2020 from the 'Gemstone' litter, after the passing of her beloved previous dog, Baxter. They share a home on the Whangaparāoa Peninsula.

It had been four years since we'd had to put down my previous dog. He was very different to Otis: he was a 50 kg Lab–mastiff cross. I'd had him since he was a tiny pup, eight or nine weeks old. My heart was shattered — losing Baxter was more devastating than my relationship breaking up. He was my best mate, and I didn't know if I could get another dog, because it's so hard when you lose them, like losing a family member.

I've always had so much love and gratitude for Helen and Gavin and what they do, even before they started the sanctuary. My previous dog never wanted to leave their kennels — they had to drag him out of the office and into my car. So when Helen and Gavin began rescuing puppies and pregnant dogs, it started me thinking. I always knew that if I got another dog I would be giving something back by rescuing one.

Otis's mum was rescued shortly before she gave birth, then Helen started posting litter pictures on Facebook, so I went up to meet them all. When I arrived, most of them were jumping around, but he was asleep in the basket, although eventually he realised people were there and got up. I was sitting next to Helen and she put a puppy in my lap. He came over and pushed the other one out, and got onto my lap instead. He did it four or five times, and

Helen said, 'Oh my god, he's picked you.'

When I first got him, he had floppy ears like a Lab; but then one day they turned into these crazy ears. He has a bit of kelpie in him, especially with the colouring. My nan wanted to call him Harry after Prince Harry, because he was a ginger, so his full name is Otis Harry Taylor.

When I got him we were in the thick of Covid, so another big deciding factor was that I knew I was going to be home a lot. But I was exhausted from looking after him; I remember sitting on the kitchen floor, and Otis was crying, and I was crying, and I rang my boss, who said, 'Take whatever time you need.' That was so great. All of a sudden he had new surroundings, so there was an adjustment period. The first month was the hardest, until he started realising, I am safe, I am not going anywhere, this is my name, this is my home.

We have a local dog park and we've formed a little dog-park family. The majority of his doggy friends are rescues as well — they're a rag-tag bunch. We've become friends outside of the park and look after each other's dogs when needed. It's nice to have that close community to call on.

He does have some quirks — one thing he does that I've never seen another dog do is he helicopter poops. He does a few turns then starts to spin around, sometimes fast, sometimes slow, then he squats to poop. Sometimes he does it, then doesn't poop. But everyone who witnesses it cracks up.

As a child, I was exposed to domestic violence through a family member, and I don't condone any kind of violence or picking on someone who can't defend themselves. Animals are not naturally violent — they will protect themselves if they need to, but they're so resilient. They can go through such trauma and stay so loving and forgiving. I was lucky with Otis because Helen saved his mother, so he didn't go through any trauma — he has only known kindness and love and safety.

Those organisations that are putting blood, sweat and tears into saving these animals need as much help as possible. What I love about Helen and Gavin is that they show the reality of animal rescue, with its ups and downs — they know that sadly they can't save them all.

Dogs are pack animals and have to be around people — you can't just let

them live alone. It breaks my heart to think about the dogs that don't get adopted, that don't get rescued and saved and rehomed. I'm really glad I did it. I knew that it was going to be a hard slog, raising a puppy and having a dog on my own, but now I can't even remember what life was like without him. He healed my heart.

Helen says:

Female dog Jewel and a male companion were found wandering the streets, having been abandoned by their owner. A compassionate couple took them in, offering them food and shelter, but as the days passed, they soon realised that even though Jewel was malnourished and neglected, she was also pregnant. Trying to find help for her, they reached out to local rescues, including our sanctuary.

With limited space, we faced a difficult decision. Collaborating with another rescue, we managed to provide a space for Jewel, recognising her dire need for care. She arrived emaciated and suffering from skin issues, her once-lustrous fur reduced to patches.

Jewel's journey towards health began with careful nourishment. We fed her small amounts every few hours, allowing her frail body to gradually regain strength. A thorough examination by our vet estimated a litter of six pups.

Jewel's labour was long and arduous, stretching through the night and into the early hours of the morning. She was exhausted, but she summoned her last reserves of strength to deliver a staggering surprise — a litter of eleven precious gems.

Already weakened by her own circumstances, Jewel could not sustain her pups, leaving us with the challenging task of hand-rearing this vulnerable litter as well as tending to the rest of the sanctuary's pups and dogs. The 'Gemstone' litter also faced their own health battles, battling constant tummy issues caused by their early hardships. However, with proper treatment and care, they grew stronger and healthier each day, and, against all odds, all eleven pups survived.

Through sleepless nights and countless hours of hand-feeding with puppy milk and electrolytes, we witnessed the resilience and fighting spirit of these precious pups, and as they blossomed into energetic, healthy beings and were adopted into their forever homes, we felt truly proud of what we had achieved.

Conclusion

A friend for life

Deciding to become a dog owner is a big decision, and one not to be taken lightly. There are many factors to consider before bringing a dog to live in your home, not least of which is the fact that it is a long-term commitment, possibly up to fifteen years. Dogs are not like cats, which are much more independent, and they're not even like children, who grow up and hopefully develop the skills they need to look after themselves. Your dog will be dependent on you for its health and happiness all its life, and you need to be prepared to take on that responsibility and give it the best possible care for all that time. In exchange, you will have the most loving and loyal companion you can imagine, who will bring endless joy, satisfaction and pleasure to your life.

If you are looking to add a dog to your family, we do hope you consider getting a rescue. In some cases, being adopted is literally the last chance for these dogs, who have done nothing to deserve the abuse and abandonment they have suffered. These dogs have so much love to give, even after coming from some tough circumstances, and every one of them deserves a second chance at life. Yes, you might need to do some extra work with an adult dog if it has experienced some trauma, and it may have some quirky habits,

but you could find you love it all the more because of that. And yes, if you adopt a rescue puppy it may have unknown parentage, and you won't know how big it will grow or what traits it may have inherited, but I know from experience that a dog's personality is much more important than its breed. Whatever your dog ends up looking like, its basic nature and how you treat it — the love you give it, and how you meet its needs for warmth, food, security and stimulation — will determine the kind of dog it grows into.

    Before bringing your dog home, you need to have made some basic arrangements so it can live comfortably with you. As well as the initial cost of buying or even adopting a dog, there are many ongoing costs to consider — not least providing it with good-quality food. It will need somewhere to rest, some toys to play with — and you will need to make the decision if it is going to sleep on the couch, or even your bed. It will take both the dog and the humans in the house a while to adjust to this new living arrangement; but by setting boundaries and being both loving and consistent, you'll find your new family member will soon feel right at home.

Bringing home a puppy and watching it grow into an adult dog is a wonderful experience, although it can be frustrating and messy in the early stages. Remember to be patient and help guide your little one as it makes mistakes and learns about the world around it. You have an amazing opportunity to shape and train this new life into a well-socialised, well-behaved and happy adult dog who can be your companion on life's adventures.

Like any animal, dogs will get sick and injured. It's your responsibility to not only take care of them when they are unwell, but also be proactive by keeping up to date with vaccinations and parasite treatments. Consistently taking care of your dog's health and well-being, including providing appropriate food and exercise and keeping its weight at a healthy level, will mean a better quality of life for the dog, and fewer trips to the vet or days and nights of worry for you.

The other aspect of taking care of your dog is making sure its behavioural needs are met. Dogs are social animals, and need interaction and exercise to keep them both mentally and physically healthy. They need to have boundaries and know what is expected of them, even if it's just basic rules and commands. A dog that knows where it stands in the family, and what it can and can't do, will feel relaxed and happy, and show its love and appreciation to you with shining eyes and a waggy tail.

As your dog passes through the various ages and stages of its life, its needs and behaviour will change, but its love for you will never waver. You will be the one constant throughout its life, and it would rather be with you than do anything else. This is an amazing privilege and an honour, and together you will form a special, unforgettable bond.

Our work at Country Retreat is a constant reminder that, even in the face of adversity, there is always hope. The dogs we work with, with their unyielding spirit, embody the resilience within us all. Their journey teaches us the power of compassion and the transformative impact of second chances.

May their stories inspire others to embrace the forgotten and broken, and to provide them with the love and care they need to thrive.

First published in 2024

Text © Helen Cook and Gavin Cook 2024
Photography © Jodie Piggott, 2024
All rights reserved. No part of this book may be reproduced or transmitted in any form or by any means, electronic or mechanical, including photocopying, recording or by any information storage and retrieval system, without prior permission in writing from the publisher.

Allen & Unwin
Level 2, 10 College Hill, Freemans Bay
Auckland 1011, New Zealand
Phone: (64 9) 377 3800
Email: auckland@allenandunwin.com
Web: www.allenandunwin.co.nz

83 Alexander Street
Crows Nest NSW 2065, Australia
Phone: (61 2) 8425 0100

A catalogue record for this book is available from the National Library of New Zealand.

ISBN 978 1 99100 666 0
Text design by Kate Barraclough
Set in Tiempos Text, Avallon and Sofia Pro
Printed in China by 1010 Printing Ltd

10 9 8 7 6 5 4 3 2 1

MIX
Paper | Supporting responsible forestry
FSC® C016973